# SMALL TRAGEDY

# SMALL TRAGEDY

## CRAIG LUCAS

THEATRE COMMUNICATIONS GROUP
NEW YORK
2018

The publication of *Small Tragedy* by Craig Lucas, through TCG's Book Program, is made possible in part by the New York State Council on the Arts with the support of Governor Andrew Cuomo and the New York State Legislature.

TCG books are exclusively distributed to the book trade by Consortium Book Sales and Distribution.

Library of Congress Control Numbers:
2017007168 (print) / 2017021834 (ebook)
ISBN 978-1-55936-507-9 (trade paper) / ISBN 978-1-55936-839-1 (ebook)
A catalog record for this book is available from the Library of Congress.

Book design and composition by Lisa Govan
Cover design by Chip Kidd
Cover painting by Brian Biedul
*Rectangle#1* in "Spaces" Series
oil on canvas, 32"x52"
www.biedul.com

First Edition, March 2018

Small Tragedy *is dedicated to*
*Deborah Eisenberg and*
*Wallace Shawn*

# PREFACE

What were the Greeks thinking? As best we can tell, they took the position that the audience was there to do the entertaining. That doesn't mean the play could be dull, discursive, dismissible. Quite the contrary. It had to be rife with the thrill of political, sexual, spiritual, personal, philosophical notions embodied in human action, such that those assembled were compelled to entertain it.

Human grasping intersects with the gods' designs, and human beings always pay the price. It is our fate. Things are beyond our control. No matter how desperately we try to avoid causing harm, we will always come to harm. Sooner or later, misfortune arrives. We are mortal.

Oedipus does every single thing in his power to do the right thing, to escape committing the terrible acts he unwittingly commits. Once he is exposed, he takes full responsibility for his action. That is tragic.

What do you call those who set forth to commit crimes, knowing full well what they are doing, then refusing to take any responsibility whatsoever?

Oedipus feels he must end the suffering of his people. The plague has befallen them and as their leader he must fix it. He does not rest until he uncovers the source of their misery.

What do you call leaders who wish to hide the source of their peoples' suffering and do not rest until they have fobbed off all blame on the sufferers themselves?

Great plays do not advocate for one side or another. They advocate for humanity, for the cost of doing the right thing and the cost of doing the wrong thing. Everyone is elevated because no one is exempt. The finger always points inward.

Athenian democracy, of course, depended on the direct participation of every citizen with a vote. They all showed up.

In the time since this play premiered in 2004, the political landscape in America has shifted unrecognizably. In a world that is wholly able to feed, clothe and protect the health and well-being of all living creatures, there should remain no justification whatsoever for battle lines over who can have enough water, food or safety.

It is also the case that the United States has become the world's greatest manufacturer of weapons and weapons-delivery systems. Those who profit most from these "products" are the ones calling the shots. As long as they can convince tribe to fight tribe, they will continue to profit, and everyone else will continue to suffer. It is in their interest that we do not get along or work toward a common good.

This tiny group of the absurdly wealthy has thus far succeeded in driving the concept of a Common Good out of public discourse altogether. It is no secret that they are so wealthy they have found, collectively, a way to *pay virtually no taxes at all* toward our common survival and to get away with doing just that: absolving themselves of any and all responsibilities other than further enriching themselves.

Our current government, by siding with these wealthiest few and demonizing all those masses of less wealthy, are working every angle to see that each demographic in our society is fighting for itself: men against women, white against black, rich against poor, entitled against disenfranchised. Them vs. Us. That m.o. will only lead to the destruction of life on Earth.

The peace process that began in the early 1960s in a corner of government that was swiftly annihilated by shadow forces built up under the OSS in the Second World War and thereafter under the CIA, FBI and the National Security apparatus in the Cold War, resulting in our shocking rush of assassinations (JFK, MLK, RFK, Malcolm X) that taught all citizens in the U.S. what was possible and what was not in our civil debate, persists. In fact, it now thrives in a vacuum.

It should be no surprise to anyone that all major print media and TV news channels maintain strong and long-standing, fully documented ties with National Security Forces. And we know what happens to anyone who ventures to critique this.

Until there is a thorough reckoning of who we are, who did what to whom and how, who continues to direct policy and by what means precisely, we will not ascend to the level of a democracy or a republic, we will remain what we have been essentially since the conclusion of the Second World War: a populace governed entirely by forces in shadow.

The immense investment of energy and time required of us all to manufacture the collective denial and willed-ignorance necessary for sustaining this peculiar reality is what *Small Tragedy* ventures to make manifest.

—*Craig Lucas*
*Putnam Valley, NY*
*January 2018*

# SMALL TRAGEDY

## PRODUCTION HISTORY

*Small Tragedy* was written during a McKnight National Residency and Commission. It had its world premiere at Playwrights Horizons (Tim Sanford, Artistic Director) in New York, on March 11, 2004. It was directed by Mark Wing-Davey. The scenic design was by Douglas Stein, the costume design was by Marina Draghici, the lighting design was by Jennifer Tipton, the music and sound design were by John Gromada; the production stage manager was Thom Widmann. The cast was:

| | |
|---|---|
| HAKIJA | Lee Pace |
| JEN | Ana Reeder |
| NATHANIEL | Rob Campbell |
| CHRISTMAS | Daniel Eric Gold |
| FANNY | Rosemarie DeWitt |
| PAOLA | Mary Shultz |

## CHARACTERS

HAKIJA

JEN

NATHANIEL TOWNSENDE III

CHRIS MASSACCIO (Christmas)

FANNY

PAOLA

## PLACE AND TIME

*Small Tragedy* takes place in Cambridge, Boston, and New York City in the mid-to-late 1990s, and in 2000.

## NOTES

When dialogue appears in columns, the conversations are simultaneous; words in **bold** are intended to take focus; it is not necessary that the subordinate conversation be understood or even entirely audible.

A slash ( / ) indicates the point in a speech or line where the subsequent speaker *may* begin overlapping; it is not imperative that he or she do so; the primary goal is verisimilitude of spontaneity as it occurs in actual conversation—unplanned, ad hoc, chaotic—that illusion of something happening for the first and only time.

An ungrammatical comma indicates a hitch in the thinking of the speaker. Pauses may be no more than grace notes. Punctuation is primarily for the reader; actors should do with it what they will.

Words in brackets are not spoken.

Nothing that is vast comes to the life of
mortals without ruin.

—SOPHOCLES


Nothing is impossible for man; what he
can't deal with he ignores.

—JACQUES LACAN

# ACT ONE

## SCENE 1

JEN: Looking back, I still couldn't say whose tragedy this is, was. Hakija's? Fanny's, Chris', Paola's, Nate's? Mine. Or if it even *is* a tragedy. Nate explained to us all once what constitutes tragedy and what is simply a very sad thing. He neglected to say whether a tragedy belongs to the participants, to those suffering, or to the people watching them suffer.

## SCENE 2

*Onstage: Paola, Jen, Nathaniel. In the corridor: Christmas and Hakija.*

PAOLA:
This is Jennifer Helburn—            NATHANIEL:
*brun*—                              Hi.
Nathaniel Townsende.

JEN: Nice to meet you.

NATHANIEL: You're readinnnnng—?

JEN AND PAOLA: Jocasta.

NATHANIEL: Anything you want to ask me?

JEN: No, I think it's pretty clear. You—?

PAOLA: I'll read Oedipus.

JEN: Okay.

PAOLA: "Jocasta, the man we sent for earlier, is that the man he means?"

JEN: . . . Sorry.

NATHANIEL: Take your time.

PAOLA: I'll give it to you again: "Jocasta, the man we sent for earlier, is that the man he means?"

JEN: "What man? Who cares what he means? Why even ask, forget it, it's not worth knowing."

PAOLA: "What? I can't stop now when I'm about to see the truth of my birth!"

JEN: "By the gods, I beg you stop! If you love your own life, stop, I've been tortured enough, haven't I?"

PAOLA: "You stop! Even if I'm discovered to be the child of slaves, you're not disgraced!"

JEN: "Please, do what I say, don't ask why!"

PAOLA: "You'll never stop me from finding out the truth."

JEN: "I want what is best for you."

PAOLA: "That is the very thing that's tormenting me."

JEN: "God help you, Oedipus, and keep the truth away from you. Secrets should be *kept*."

PAOLA: "Someone go find the shepherd, let my wife take pride in her nobility."

JEN: "Goodbye, my poor, deluded, lost, cursed, those are the last names I'll ever give you."

NATHANIEL: Good. Very good. Nice.

JEN: Thanks.

NATHANIEL: Thanks. Very much.

JEN: It's been a long time since I've auditioned.

NATHANIEL: No, that was wonderful, thank you.

JEN: Weren't—? I think I missed you at Yale by one year.

NATHANIEL: Oh. Yeah? Are you Equity?

JEN: No, long story. I—I'm just finally getting back to it.

NATHANIEL: Well, thank you.

JEN: Can I do another speech?

NATHANIEL:

| | |
|---|---|
| Well, | PAOLA: |
| we're on a tight— | I think— |

JEN: Please? I'll be quick.

NATHANIEL: Sure. *(To Paola)* It's okay. / You're great. I love you.

JEN: This is the Messenger, right after . . . Well . . .

"Jocasta's dead: her own hand.
You weren't there, you can't know how horrible it was.
I was. I was there. She burst in, our queen,
Now demented and wringing her hair,
Running through doors, running, then locks herself in the
bedroom, crying:
'Laius! Here is our bed! Soiled.
Filthy *soil* bringing forth a husband by a husband,
And children by a child! All soiled.
We made love!' . . . Which we does she mean?

We move—But then the son, husband, king, prince, raving,
stamping up and down, bellows:
'A weapon! Now! Where is she? Find me that double breeding ground!
*Where?*'
And hurls himself against the door, again, breaking the bolts,
falling to his knees before: Wife . . . mother . . . hanging by
the neck, twisted.

11

He removes her golden brooches, fingering them,
Holding them up,
Then rams the long pins into:
'Wicked, wicked eyes! You'll never know,
Never know my shame,
Go dark for all time,
Blind to what you should not have seen,'

Now? This chant goes up: 'Loved her, loved her,'
Each time striking once more, deep in, dripping, oozing bloody
muck,
'Loved her, loved her.'

Such happiness.
Once. Now: 'Catastrophe!
Throw wide the doors.
Let all Thebes see, father-killer, mother . . . No, too rank to say.
I AM THE PLAGUE!
I AM THE PLAGUE!
I AM THE PLAGUE!'
Look. The gates are opening."

I thought I should . . . familiarize myself with what she goes
through . . . you know . . . if I was going to actually play the
part. Anyway . . . It's a beautiful translation.

*(Paola and Jen exit into the corridor.)*

PAOLA: Chris Massaccio?
CHRISTMAS: Right.
JEN: Good luck.
CHRISTMAS: Thanks.

*(Christmas and Paola go onstage. Jen and Hakija remain in
the corridor. Jen is upset.)*

PAOLA: Chris Masssssssacio, Nathaniel Townsende.

CHRISTMAS: Hey.

NATHANIEL: Christmas?

CHRISTMAS: No. Chris Massaccio.

| HAKIJA: | NATHANIEL: |
|---|---|
| Sorry. | Oh, oh. |

JEN: I'm sorry.

NATHANIEL: Did you want to ask me anything?

CHRISTMAS: Yeah, I did.

HAKIJA: Didn't go well?

| CHRISTMAS: | JEN: |
|---|---|
| Uh—Oh, yeah, fate | It went really well. I'm sorry— |
| NATHANIEL: | |
| Yes. | |
| | —forgive me. |

CHRISTMAS: But—

JEN: Oh god.

*(Jen exits.)*

CHRISTMAS: —I mean, I don't believe that, do you, that things are predetermined?

NATHANIEL: Neither do they, they thought they were *fated*, big difference, but it doesn't matter what I believe, they believed it.

CHRISTMAS: But how do you make sense out of the play, then— like now?

NATHANIEL: *Like* now? Youuuu believe it while you're doing it.

CHRISTMAS: But still that leaves the audience going, "What the hell does this have to do with me?" / And what—?

NATHANIEL: Well, b / ut—

PAOLA: We're running about—

NATHANIEL: By that logic, I'm, you're not wrong, it's a very good question, but you couldn't get anything from *Hamlet*, we don't believe in ghosts.

13

CHRISTMAS: Oh, I do. You don't believe in ghosts?

NATHANIEL:
Well, if—Look. Have you never found
yourself doing things the same way you
did them before even though they didn't
work then and it makes no sense
for you to do it that way,
dating someone who                               CHRISTMAS:
is really terrible—Well, there you go—        Ugh.
And in the *same way* the last really
terrible person for you—                          Yes . . .
. . .                                                           don't even get
Is that not a kind of fate?                        [me—]
Some things defy reason:

CHRISTMAS: Yes.

NATHANIEL: War, drug addiction, my nose hair, these forces, smile please, deep, thank you, within us—

CHRISTMAS: Yes.

PAOLA: I think we have to . . .

NATHANIEL: To be continued. Okay, you're reading . . .

CHRISTMAS: Oh, um. Priest, Messenger—

NATHANIEL: Good.

CHRISTMAS: Herdsman, Soothsayer Guy, I'm sweating like a feckin' pig here.

NATHANIEL: I see.

CHRISTMAS: We're not supposed to take work outside the theater department, so, but—

NATHANIEL: Well, if you're—

CHRISTMAS: No, no, I'm sick of carrying spears, you know what I mean? Anyway, okay.

*(He begins his audition [see Appendix A]. Fanny arrives in the corridor.)*

FANNY: Are these the auditions? . . . Is it just the two of us? . . . What version did you bring? I'm sorry, are you preparing?

HAKIJA: It's okay.

FANNY: Oh god, did I bring the wrong one? Did it say that?

HAKIJA: It's the best I could find.

FANNY: How could you tell? Where are you from? You sound like you have an accent?

HAKIJA: Where does it sound like I'm from?

FANNY: I don't know, Russia? . . . I have to guess.

HAKIJA: You could leave it a mystery.

FANNY: Oh, okay, uh . . . Romania? Uhhhh, Yugoslavia? *(Hakija nods)* . . . Yay! Isn't there, but, like a, sort of a [like] *war* there?

HAKIJA: There is very much a war there.

FANNY: Oh. Is that why you're here? I'm sorry, I'm terribly nervous, this is the first time I've ever auditioned for a play set in *"olden"* times, I usually do newish, you know, contemporary things, so . . . It helps to think about someone else, you want a shot? It's just wine, that's the only way I can get through these. I'm going to wind up like some old . . . So tell me about your family, are they here too?

HAKIJA: What if I were to tell you they were all dead?

FANNY: Oh. My god, I'm sorry.

HAKIJA: I said, "What if I *were* to tell you?"

FANNY: Oh. Well . . . Are they? I mean . . . *What?*

HAKIJA: Myyyy . . . mother and father are here.

FANNY: Oh good. Good for you. In Boston?

HAKIJA: My father and I lived for many years innnn . . . *Vermont.*

FANNY: Oh, you've been here, I see. You're American. American Yugoslav.

HAKIJA: He is a carpenter. I was schooled at home.

FANNY: Oh. I, this, I really appreciate your talking to me, the less I think about this . . . You're not like Bosnian.

HAKIJA: I am.

FANNY: Isn't that [where]—? You speak beautiful English, the accent is very very faint.

HAKIJA: Most Europeans learn to speak English in their youth, even if I had grown up there.

FANNY: Yugoslavia is part of Europe? *(Pause)* So . . . just you and your father, what happened to your mother? Did you say?

HAKIJA: My mother, I was told, abandoned me.

FANNY: Ohhhh.

HAKIJA: He's a taciturn fellow, my father, and rarely spoke except when teaching me. I was allowed to have friends over, but only when he was there, and I was not permitted to visit other people's homes or watch TV—

FANNY: Really?

HAKIJA: Well, we didn't have one, not even a radio. No newspapers.

FANNY: Wow. Did you, I don't know, go to church?

HAKIJA: Technically we are Muslims but my father is atheist, I am an atheist.

FANNY: I didn't know there were atheist Muslims.

PAOLA *(To those in the corridor)*: I'm sorry we're running so late, does anyone have to leave right away?

FANNY: Not me.

*(Paola returns to the stage as Christmas reads the new speech.)*

Go on.

HAKIJA: I must have beennnnn, twelve, just, when he went to collect a piece of furniture, and I sneaked to a friend's house. My friend's mother asked if I wanted a glass of milk, and as she was pouring I saw a face of a boy on the milk carton, and a name, not mine, but a common Bosnian name, and my friend's mother asked what was wrong. Two days later a sheriff arrived and arrested my father for kidnapping.

FANNY: No.

HAKIJA: He was not my father at all, but a man living in an area of Detroit inhabited by many other Muslims—

FANNY: No.

HAKIJA: —and he saw my mother abusing me; she was a drunk and a pothead—I know, because I was returned to her, given my old name—

FANNY: Is this—?

HAKIJA: She fell asleep smoking and burned half of our house down. Among other things. And my "father" was sent to prison where he is still serving a sentence.

FANNY:
Oh. My.
Go—

CHRISTMAS *(A snippet)*:
"Catastrophe! Throw wide the doors—"

HAKIJA:
He'd wanted a child, saw me in danger, sold all of his possessions, snatched me, drove as far north as he could go near the border, bought a small tract of land, and—

. . .

. . .

She, of course, would not let me go visit him; I couldn't tell her I loved him.

FANNY: Did you love her? Too? . . .

HAKIJA: When I turned sixteen, I told her I was going to visit him in Attica whether she liked it or not; she just stood there like a stone statue with tears draining from it, and then whispered, "Let me send him a package, will you take it to him?" I told him I loved him and missed him and didn't blame him; he'd never abused me, he was my true father, she was a bad dream: invention of fate. I gave him the heavy paper sack, he opened it, never speaking a word, we parted, I ran away from home, came here.

CHRISTMAS: "... you may see for yourselves. Look: the gates are / opening."

FANNY:
Good ...
... *god.*

NATHANIEL:
Good. Great. Very very nice. Really. We're running a little late—

CHRISTMAS:
Sure, sure, okay, thanks, good luck, / thanks. I mean—

PAOLA:
*(Entering corridor)* Hajika?

NATHANIEL:
Thanks.

HAKIJA:
Hakija.

CHRISTMAS *(As he goes out)*:
You're welcome.

PAOLA: Hakija, sorry. Whenever you're ready. Sorry we're so behind.

*(Paola returns to the stage.)*

FANNY: Break a leg.

HAKIJA: Thank you.

FANNY: Can I ask ... What was in the paper bag?

HAKIJA: Oh. Horseshit, like the rest of the story. See you.

*(Hakija goes onstage.)*

CHRISTMAS: Good luck with your audition. Mine sucked the big wet one.

## SCENE 3

*Jen and Fanny's apartment.*

FANNY: "Horseshit. Just like the rest of the story. See you." . . . You think that's funny?

| JEN: | |
|---|---|
| Yeah. Isn't | FANNY: |
| it? | Never mind. |
| I'm sorry, it . . . | . . . |
| W—? | I thought it was real, I was upset for |
| . . . | him. |
| I'm sorry, you're right, | . . . |
| I see . . . | Was I . . . ? Maybe I don't have a |
| . . . | sense of humor, he was very very very |
| . . . | very creepoid. |

It sounds it. *(Pause)* But . . . I still think it's funny.

FANNY: I was vulnerable, I was about—

*(Phone rings.)*

Hello? No, wait, what number did you think you were—? *(Hangs up)* They were in a fucking hurry, I was vulnerable, I was nervous, I was about to go in to audition, it's like . . .

| | JEN: |
|---|---|
| FANNY: | You're, |
| . . . it was my mother's | you're right. |
| funeral and he came up to me | . . . |
| and kicked me in the groin or | . . . |
| something. | Well . . . yeah, not . . . quite. |
| . . . | |
| Look, no offense— | |

JEN: How much have you had?

FANNY: Don't do that, it's just wine. Some.

JEN:
You've had *some*? Oh.
*Some.*
. . .
. . .
Which
people?
I married one bad man,
that doesn't . . .

FANNY:
You, are not, a reliable, judge of
people, I think history bears this
out. You are drawn to these people.
. . .
Bad, bad people, bad men.

FANNY: And what does that say about me, anyway, why did you pick me?

JEN: Because you're bad?

FANNY: Why didn't you just . . . ? You're seven years older than me, why didn't you get your own place?

JEN: I'm broke. You think I have terrible / judgment.

FANNY: They're not gonna call, they're not gonna call, I can't act. Why am I going to grad school? Why don't I just . . . sign my life over to Wendy's?

*(She turns on the TV. It's the news; she flips the channels.)*

Look at all of these actors, they're all working, they're all getting paid, they're all beautiful or quirkily beautiful or related to someone famous and here I am waiting in knots in a tenement fucking apartment in the suburbs of Boston to find out if I can be allowed to please play an Elder for no money in an amateur production of a two-million-year-old play. I mean, did you *read* it?

JEN: *Oedipus*? I've, well, I've read it before.

FANNY: "I've read it before."

JEN: Can we stop this?

FANNY: I mean, I don't know why we're supposed to like him, seriously. I don't want to be in it. If I think about it. Do I?

JEN: You don't have to like him, you have to feel terror and pity.

FANNY: Well, okay, then, why pity? Where's the pity? What's it for? He kills people who get in his way.

JEN: Yeah, but the gods shit all over him.

FANNY: So where's *our* play then?

JEN: I never know why people do mean things, though. I couldn't understand how Bart could be so mean about paying alimony after he was dumping *me*.

FANNY: Money and comfort, that's all everybody wants really.

JEN: Is that really true / though?

*(Phone rings.)*

FANNY: Hello? . . . Just a sec.

JEN: Hi? . . . Oh. Oh, great, wow. Thanks. Six thirty?, tomorrow?, sure, great, yeah, I know where it is. Thanks a lot. Bye.

FANNY: Your dentist?

JEN: I got the part.

FANNY: Great. Good. I'm really really really really happy.

JEN: Okay.

FANNY: I said I was happy.

JEN: Okay.

FANNY: You can only expect so much of people.

JEN: I said / okay—

FANNY: I am not *acting* on my desire to hurt you. I don't want to play an Elder.

*(Phone rings.)*

Hello? This is she. Oh, great. Which, um, I mean, how many Elders are there going to be in the Chorus? Thanks, bye. That's *First Elder* to you.

## SCENE 4

*Onstage. Hakija, Jen, Fanny, Christmas—who has just arrived from class, breathless, not yet settled—Paola, and Nathaniel.*

FANNY: "*Oedipus the Tyrant*, a new English adaptation from Sophocles by Nathaniel Townsende III. In front of the palace of Oedipus at . . ."

NATHANIEL: Thebes.

FANNY: Right. "Two generations before the Trojan War. To the right of the stage near the altar stands the Priest with a crowd of / Thebans."

NATHANIEL: Thebans.

FANNY: Very good. "Oedipus emerges from the central door."

HAKIJA: "Children, what are you doing here, pleading, bent down?" Children?

NATHANIEL: They're implied . . . out there, the audience, children, hoping for easy entertainment, reaching up toward the light. *Kelp*, as it were. Imagine them waving in a deep pool, their lives lived in darkness. Whenever. Sorry.

HAKIJA: "The city is burdened with moans, incense, intertwined, I wouldn't trust a messenger, so came— . . . Ah, so came to see with my own king's eyes." Turns to Priest? "You speak for them?"

CHRISTMAS: "Our ship, the city of Thebes, can barely lift her prow—"

NATHANIEL: Prow.

CHRISTMAS:
"—*prow* from these bloody waves:
Plague dragging our, dragging down our people,
drowning them in death.
You saved our city once.
You rid of

CHRISTMAS *(cont.)*:
us the cursed—"
...
Where should I—?

NATHANIEL:
"Once *before*." "You rid *us* of—"
Take your time.

NATHANIEL: "You saved our city once before." And actually it's,
"Our city, the ship of Thebes."

CHRISTMAS: "You saved our city once. Before. You rid . . . of us,"
it says.

NATHANIEL: That's a typo.

CHRISTMAS: "You rid ooooo-us of the cursed Sphinx with the
help of the gods, some say,
And we beseech thee, help us once more.
If you don't, you will rule over a cit—an empty city."

NATHANIEL: Great.

HAKIJA: "Yes, how I pity you, come filled with such wanting,
I know what is happening, for I bear the sorrow of you all,
I cannot sleep nor think of . . . but else.
I have sent Creon,
My brother-in-law, to the oracle.
He will learn how I may save this city.
He's been gone a long time.
When he returns, I swear I will do what gods command,
or call me a villain and send me into exile."

CHRISTMAS:                     FANNY:
"He comes."                    Foreshadow— *(Pause)* —ing, / sorry.

NATHANIEL: See him first? Maybe?

CHRISTMAS: "He comes."

HAKIJA: "Creon?"

CHRISTMAS: "He looks pretty happy."

HAKIJA: "Brother, what news?"

NATHANIEL: "It is the guilt of murder that plagues our city.
We must drive out the polluted killer."

HAKIJA: "Well, who might he be? Are there clues as to his where-
abouts?"

NATHANIEL: "The clues are here, right here before us, according to the gods."

HAKIJA: "Where did he die, the king?"

NATHANIEL: "He went by himself, never returned."

HAKIJA: "Was there no messenger, no traveling companion?"

NATHANIEL: "All killed, save one."

HAKIJA: "One?"

NATHANIEL: "He ran in fright, told us but one thing."

HAKIJA: "Which was?"

NATHANIEL: "That there were many robbers, many hands committeth the murder. How could these robbers have not backers from the city?"

FANNY:
"Creon shrugs."

NATHANIEL:
"The—" You don't have to read those. Thanks. You are *diligent*! "The Sphinx and her damned riddles kept us too busy to be solving crimes."

HAKIJA:
"I will bring light to this darkness."

NATHANIEL:
*"Exit all but the Chorus."*
Now, go very slowly with this, the way I've broken it up—

FANNY:
*"Exit all . . ."*

PAOLA: All right, all right.

NATHANIEL: Fanny?

FANNY: What?

NATHANIEL: Do you understand how it's divided?

FANNY: We'll see.

PAOLA: "What does it mean?"

PAOLA AND FANNY: "What does it all mean? Gods, speak."

PAOLA:
"Athena—"

FANNY:
"A—" That's me. But can I just ask?

FANNY *(cont.)*:
What do . . . ? Are we two people?
Do we represent . . . more . . . people?

NATHANIEL: Well. That's a really good question.

FANNY: Oh. Well, I feel better, thank you, but—what's the answer?

PAOLA:                   NATHANIEL:
Maybe—                 Let's— Let's explore it as we go, all
                              right? Not jump to—The most
FANNY:                   powerful place artistically is *not*
Oh.                         *knowing* . . . Seriously. Out of that
                              everything else grows.

FANNY: You sound like the Buddha. "The power of not knowing."

NATHANIEL: I'm being serious. Look, I mean, I could tell you—

FANNY: / No—

NATHANIEL: "The play's about this, the play's about that," do this, do that, but what good would that be?

FANNY: I was just—

NATHANIEL: You'd be doing it for me. But you're not here to please me, you're here to please yourself.

FANNY: Right.

NATHANIEL: Do you understand?

FANNY: No.

NATHANIEL: You don't?

FANNY: No, but I'm slow, it's not you.

NATHANIEL: Would you like it if I were to answer everything for you, tell you where to stand and sit and interpret the whole play?

FANNY: Sure.

NATHANIEL: Okay.

FANNY: Go on? "Athena, immortal daughter of Zeus:"

PAOLA: "And Artemis, also daughter of Zeus, overseer of all wild things:"

FANNY AND PAOLA: "Forests, beasts, barbarians, women."

PAOLA: I'm sorry, Nate.

NATHANIEL:
Can we—?
I just want to hear it. All ri—?

PAOLA:
But—I know, but I've
compared the other
available translations—

This is an adaptation.

PAOLA: No, I know, but—"beasts, barbarians, *women*—?"

NATHANIEL:
That was the attitude at
the time. Let's just—
It's a free adaptation and
the text is not up for discussion.
Not now.

PAOLA:
It isn't in Sophocles.
Lloyd-Jones has—

PAOLA: Then . . . Oh, fine. You don't want to hear?

NATHANIEL: No, you think, what, that I didn't bother to look at
the other translations—

PAOLA: / No.

NATHANIEL:
I mean, all the other—?!?, before
I settled on this—you think I just,
what—?, pulled it all out of my ass?

PAOLA:
No.

PAOLA: No, I—Never mind.

NATHANIEL: No, go on, you've broken the rhythm—we might as
well—

PAOLA: You have Oedipus saying, "You cannot think of *butt* else."
You have the Priest saying, "He looks pretty happy!" It soun-
deth silly, honey.

NATHANIEL: I don't think it will sound "silly" in fact I know it
won't once it's played for its truth, there's deep feeling under
every moment. Let's take a break.

PAOLA: No, no, I said it, look, my name isn't going on it, I'll say
whatever you ask me to say.

NATHANIEL:
I really, this, I mean, if this is
your attitude on the first day,      PAOLA:
the first hour—                      I only, if you don't
. . .                                understand I'm trying
. . .                                to save you humiliation—
We're taking a break.

PAOLA: I'm in your corner, Nate, I've said it—

NATHANIEL: Come outside with me.

PAOLA:
No. I'm through—                     NATHANIEL:
I'm through, if you want advice,     Now? Please? Would you?
I'll give it, otherwise I'll shut up.

NATHANIEL: I'm not asking anyone to shut up.

PAOLA: Well, I am. "Forests, beasts, barbarians, women."

FANNY: Go on?

PAOLA AND FANNY: "And lastly, Apollo:
    Purifier, ideal of young male beauty, watcher over music,
    archery, prophecy,
    Medicine and the care of flocks and herds.
    Hear us, you three preventers of fate!"

NATHANIEL: Paola.

*(Paola might laugh and lose some words:)*

PAOLA AND FANNY: "Our woes are infinite,
    The ship of state is made of rotten wood.
    No children are born, there is only death."

NATHANIEL: You're fucking fired.

PAOLA: Good luck everybody!

NATHANIEL: Paola—

PAOLA: Those goddamn beasts and women, you know!

*(Paola exits.)*

NATHANIEL: Come back, I don't mean it, it's—Why doesn't every-body go for a ... ?

*(He exits.)*

CHRISTMAS: Wheeeeeeeeeee.

HAKIJA: You got the part.

JEN: The ... ?

HAKIJA: You got the part.

CHRISTMAS: I wonder if it's / going to be like this ...

JEN: What do you mean?

HAKIJA: You were upset about your audition.

JEN *(To Fanny, mouthed)*: *What? (To Hakija)* No. I was upset because it was good. I haven't acted in seven years.

HAKIJA: No?

JEN: I gave it up for somebody who seemed to need me much more than I needed it, I thought, and after I put him through the rest of medical school, I took a job as a pharmacist's assistant which I am *still* doing, believe it or not, he dumps me for his, ladies and germs, his secretary whom he had impregnated, and at that point I was actually pregnant after trying for seven *years.* So I had an abortion and here we find ourselves at ... What shall we call this? Skit Night in Dixie.

HAKIJA: Not so funny.

JEN: Well, no.

HAKIJA: You make a joke.

*(Paola and Nathaniel return.)*

NATHANIEL: Okay, we're back. Look, everyone, it isn't that I don't want your feedback, I do, your suggestions, but not—Come to me individually, all right? *(To Paola)* You okay?

PAOLA: Just go on.

NATHANIEL: That way we won't be taking up the other actors' time hammering out changes. But I want your thoughts, your questions, this is a collective process, and I believe foremost in process. We're going to discover, *together*, what this thing is. So, let's start with Oedipus's next speech.

FANNY: We didn't finish our—

NATHANIEL: Oh, yes, right, the Chorus, from . . .

FANNY: "In the countless deaths—" *(To Paola)* You ready? "In the countless"

FANNY AND PAOLA: "*deaths.*"

FANNY: "The children born without"

PAOLA AND FANNY: "*breath.*"

FANNY: "Cold from the"

FANNY AND PAOLA: "*womb.*"

FANNY: "White-haired women and wives bend to you with prayer:"

FANNY AND PAOLA: "Save us!

Our enemy is Zeus,

Drive him out, drive him back!

Banish Zeus from our hometown!"

NATHANIEL: *What?*

PAOLA: Honey, Zeus isn't the, no, I'm sorry, we'll talk about it later—

NATHANIEL: Zeus, isn't the *what*?, please?, I'm asking you.

PAOLA: I thought . . . You've misread, Zeus isn't the enemy, King Laius's killer is the enemy, Zeus is being called on to get rid of the jerk. I mean . . .

NATHANIEL: All right, we'll look at it. I am perfectly capable of admitting that I can make a mistake. Clearly.

PAOLA: What does that mean?

NATHANIEL: "*Oedipus returns.*"

| HAKIJA: | FANNY: |
|---|---|
| "The thing—" | "*Oedipus—*" |
| . . . | Sorry. |
| "The—" | "*Oedipus returns.*" |

HAKIJA *(cont.)*:
"[The] thing you ask of me,
if you will hear and embrace my words,
fight the plague with me,
you will discover the courage to banish all this suffering . . .
I am a stranger to this story and to this act of murder.
If any man knows whose hand it was that slayeth Laius—
Slayeth Laius . . ."
NATHANIEL: Slayed Laius. No, that . . . felled . . . "If any man knows
whose hand it was that . . ."
HAKIJA: "—slaughtered the king . . ."
NATHANIEL: "—slaughtered the . . . slaughtered *Laius*, no slaugh-
tered the king . . ."
HAKIJA: "—slaughtered Laius—"
NATHANIEL: Okay?
HAKIJA: "I, I am a stranger to this story and to this murderous act.
If any man—"
NATHANIEL: "This act of—" No, that's better, you're right, sorry,
go on.
HAKIJA: "If any man knows whose hand it was that slaughtered
Laius, I command him speak."
NATHANIEL: Him, good, Hajika.
HAKIJA:
Hakija.
"And if he is afraid to incriminate          NATHANIEL:
himself, I promise no bitter punishment:    God, fuck, I even
He may *depart* our city unharmed."         practiced it.
NATHANIEL: Depart, better.
PAOLA: Christ.
NATHANIEL: Sh.

*(Paola exits during:)*

HAKIJA:
"If he knows the killer to
be a foreigner,
I command him speak.

But if he keeps silence,
To protect himself or a friend,
For any reason,
Here is what I shall do:"
...
...
...
"Here—Here is what I shall do:
Hear me!
May he be banished, driven out, *unseen*,
his life in exile, cursed everywhere he goes."

NATHANIEL:
Paola ... Paola ...
Oh great ...
...
...
Go on. You're doing
wonderfully.
Really.
Wonderfully. Sorry.

NATHANIEL: He's cursing himself!

HAKIJA: "Whoever did this deed, know that you are never to be
at home anywhere,
Always to wander, filthy and abhorred.
And if I should learn he lives in the confines of *my own home*,
May *I then* be so cursed, banished, doomed! Yes!
Since I now wear his crown
And have his queen for my wife—"

*(Paola reenters.)*

PAOLA: What is so patently disgusting to me—
NATHANIEL: Out.

PAOLA:
Is that I have to save up my
suggestions for bettering the text
but this one gets to suggest
anything he likes, it is so
transparent how much you

NATHANIEL:
Paola. *Paola* ...
Okay. Great.

31

PAOLA *(cont.)*:
want to blow him, why don't
you just get down on your knees
now and we can all get it over
with. You moron, you hypocrite,
you asked me to help you.
. . .
His dick is this big.

NATHANIEL *(cont.)*:
Go . . .
You're humiliating
no one but . . .
. . .

*(Door slam!)*

## SCENE 5

*Bus. Fanny and Jen.*

FANNY: That was him.
JEN: Who?
FANNY: Oedipus. The guy who told me that story. At the audition.
JEN: Oh.
FANNY: Worrisome, no?
JEN: No. Yeah.

*(Add: a bar. Christmas and Hakija.)*

CHRISTMAS: This okay?
JEN: What was it again?
FANNY:
"Horseshit, just like the
rest of the story."
Weren't you listening when I . . . ?

JEN:
Right right.

JEN: No, I was, it's, I mean—
CHRISTMAS: That's okay.
JEN: —you have to admit—

HAKIJA: You sure?

JEN:

—that was some major horseshit

tonight, that's all.          CHRISTMAS:

I'm thinking.          You get the next one.

          HAKIJA:

          Okay.

FANNY: You were never away from him long enough to tell you.

JEN: I wasn't? Well, there wasn't anywhere to go. That theater is where we go when we die if we've been bad.

FANNY: Too late to back out?

JEN: No.

CHRISTMAS: Man.

JEN: Not at all. I would if . . . No, not at / all.

FANNY: If you were me?

JEN: No no.

FANNY: Why me?

CHRISTMAS: That was . . .

JEN: I don't know, I didn't say that. Because, well, you have two lines.

HAKIJA: Yeah.

JEN: At least I'm playing, I mean, look, the whole thing is nuts.

FANNY: You think I should quit.

JEN: No.

HAKIJA: Funny.

JEN: I was, *I* would probably—

CHRISTMAS: Shit.

JEN: Yes. I don't know, I'm not you, though.

CHRISTMAS: Do you think the translation is so bad?

HAKIJA: No.

CHRISTMAS: Me either.

FANNY: There is something very . . .

CHRISTMAS: And . . .

FANNY: . . . *very* wrong with that guy.

JEN: Nate?

CHRISTMAS:
Are they
a couple?
...
I think he's sort of sexy.
...
I'd do him.
...
I'm not exactly clear on how
he sees the play, but...
...
Are you?

JEN:
Oh. Yeah. Good actor,
though. *(Pause)* But—
...
...yeah, he is... very...
...
intense, kind of.
...
...
That's sort of the part
...
though.

HAKIJA: I'm not sure he is either.

CHRISTMAS: So... You're... Where are you from? Originally?

HAKIJA: Bosnia.

CHRISTMAS: Yeowch.

JEN: ... Are you mad at me?

FANNY: Why?

CHRISTMAS: Sorry.

JEN: 'Cause I said I would quit?

FANNY: No.

CHRISTMAS: I mean...

FANNY: Just don't sleep with him.

JEN: Please.

CHRISTMAS: Wow.

JEN: Or because I didn't... remember...

FANNY: No. Please.

CHRISTMAS: Glad you're here.

FANNY: I'm not that...

CHRISTMAS: And not there.

*(Add: Nathaniel's apartment. Nathaniel and Paola.)*

NATHANIEL: Paola?

JEN: You're sure?

NATHANIEL: Paola?

CHRISTMAS: How long? You . . . been here?

HAKIJA: Six months.

NATHANIEL: Let me in.

CHRISTMAS: Are . . . ? Can I ask?

NATHANIEL: Honey?

CHRISTMAS: Are . . . ? You're straight, right?

HAKIJA: Americans think it makes people less mysterious if you give them a name.

CHRISTMAS: You're right.

JEN: Thanks.

CHRISTMAS: We do.

HAKIJA: Your movies and books all purport to explain human beings.

NATHANIEL: I'm pouring a drink, do you want one?

HAKIJA: You can't explain human beings.

CHRISTMAS: Here's to that.

PAOLA: I hate you.

CHRISTMAS: To mystery!

NATHANIEL: I'm aware.

HAKIJA: Tchin-tchin.

NATHANIEL: Here's your drink. You've already had some, haven't you?

PAOLA: Fuck you.

NATHANIEL: All right. If that'll fix it.

PAOLA: No— You cast that . . . *milkmaid* as Jocasta, she was *fine* as the Messenger, but . . . You wouldn't even let me see the script, I'm so—

NATHANIEL: I know.

PAOLA: —*humiliated.*

NATHANIEL: I'm sorry.

PAOLA: Why did you do that?

NATHANIEL: I just wanted to hear it once without a lot of criticism.

*(Pause.)*

CHRISTMAS: But are you?

PAOLA: I'll be good.

CHRISTMAS: I mean—

PAOLA: I felt so exposed.

CHRISTMAS: You don't have to . . .

PAOLA: I'm the only Equity actor there—

CHRISTMAS: I mean, I'm not trying to explain you.

PAOLA: —I'm supposed to be your co-director, you didn't mention that to anyone—

FANNY: I think it could be good.

JEN: You do?

PAOLA: —you so obviously found that child—

FANNY: I do.

PAOLA: —I don't know—

NATHANIEL: I didn't, though—

JEN: Yeah.

NATHANIEL: —you imagined that.

JEN: Maybe.

PAOLA: Whatever.

CHRISTMAS: To mystery!

PAOLA: Cheers.

JEN: It could, I think.

PAOLA: You just tell me what you want, you know I'll do it.

NATHANIEL: No, we're partners.

PAOLA: No, we're not.

NATHANIEL: Yes.

PAOLA: No.

JEN: Let's stick in there for a while.

NATHANIEL: Yes.

FANNY: Why not?

JEN: What the hell.

PAOLA: No. "Banish Zeus from our *hometown*?"

NATHANIEL: That was awkward. Our city?

CHRISTMAS: Did you think I was? Straight or . . . ? Bi?

PAOLA: . . . It'll be a very beautiful production—

CHRISTMAS: No.

PAOLA: People are terrified—

CHRISTMAS: No—

PAOLA: —of Greek tragedy—

CHRISTMAS: I don't want to know.

PAOLA: —you'll throw them against the wall and nail them.

CHRISTMAS: Seriously. Here's to mystery. I mean it!

PAOLA: Right here. In your own hometown.

NATHANIEL: Shut up.

PAOLA: . . . I'm glad you're finally doing something.

*(Pause.)*

NATHANIEL: Yeah. Can we be? Please? Partners?

PAOLA: Oh, of course. I'm sorry.

NATHANIEL: They'll see I don't know anything.

PAOLA: Of course you know something.

HAKIJA: So . . .

PAOLA: I love you.

HAKIJA: You're dyslexic.

NATHANIEL: I love you, too.

CHRISTMAS: You could tell?

NATHANIEL: God.

## SCENE 6

*Rehearsal. All assembled.*

NATHANIEL: Listen up. New pages. As I've said, we'll continue to get stuff as my co-adaptor and co-director and I—

PAOLA: Okay.

NATHANIEL: —work our way through the text. Your patience is hugely appreciated, again: process, process, process; you are an immensely talented crew, and we are, both of us, more excited than we may appear at having you all collaborate with us, dig, seek out the deeper truth in this . . .

PAOLA: Et cetera.

NATHANIEL:
Okay. Page . . .
whatever, help me . . .
someone . . .
/ fucking . . . Why don't I have an—

JEN:
Pretty blouse. Really really—

CHRISTMAS:
You motherfucker. Joke.
/ Mother—

PAOLA *(Mocking Nathaniel)*:
Sixteen. You do have an.

NATHANIEL:
Okay— This is one of those
places where the condensation
is most severe: I want this production to feel
like a bullet going right into the wound,
not only making it but flying out
the other side and splattering
the wall with the audience's guts
and brains.

HAKIJA:
Got it.

FANNY: Yum.

NATHANIEL: Where we left off.

FANNY: "Teiresias, the blind prophet of Apollo."

HAKIJA: "Yes, I have sent for him."

FANNY: "Here he comes: the only man—"

PAOLA AND FANNY: "Here he comes: the only man for whom truth is second nature."

NATHANIEL: I don't think he wears a blindfold.

CHRISTMAS: I'm trying to figure out what it's like to / be—

NATHANIEL: Good. Great, good idea.

HAKIJA: "Teiresias, you see more than any other man, though you are blind.

Spare us none of your knowledge,

Save us, save your city,

Save me."

NATHANIEL: Good.

CHRISTMAS: "Knowledge is worthless if save you it can't."

NATHANIEL: "—if it cannot save you."

CHRISTMAS: "If it cannot save you." Sorry. "I knew this—"

NATHANIEL: I know.

CHRISTMAS: No, that's the line. "I knew this, but tried to know it not—"

NATHANIEL: *Un*know it, no "not."

CHRISTMAS: "Unknow it, no . . ." "I knew this—"

NATHANIEL: Take a break everyone, we'll work on this for a bit—

CHRISTMAS: "I knew this, / but tried to—"

NATHANIEL: —then resume, ask Paola questions, this is all good, great work. I mean it, really, you're all incredible. Okay. It's fine.

CHRISTMAS: I know.

NATHANIEL: Breathe.

CHRISTMAS: I'll get it.

NATHANIEL: Christmas.

CHRISTMAS: I will, I promise.

NATHANIEL: *Merry* Christmas.

CHRISTMAS: Ho ho.

NATHANIEL: Have some fun.

CHRISTMAS: Oh.

NATHANIEL: You didn't have any problem at the audition.

CHRISTMAS: I'd memorized it, that's all, I'll memorize this.

NATHANIEL: Okay.

JEN *(Approaches Hakija)*: So . . .

CHRISTMAS: This always happens.

NATHANIEL: Is there anything I'm doing that—?

JEN: Oh.

CHRISTMAS: No no no no no.

NATHANIEL: Or anything you'd like me to?

JEN: Thanks.

CHRISTMAS: No. I mean . . . I'd love to . . . have a drink with you some night but—

JEN: Great.

NATHANIEL: Sure. Sure sure sure. Of course. Let's . . .

JEN: You, uh . . .

NATHANIEL: Let's just read it slowly, all right?

FANNY *(To Paola)*: So you worked / on the translation?

*(Hakija offers Jen a bite of his food.)*

JEN: No thanks. / Thanks.

HAKIJA: Hm?

FANNY: How long have you known Nate?

JEN: You know . . .

PAOLA: We met during the Pleistocene.

JEN: You kind of—

FANNY: Is that a Greek play?

JEN: —you kind of freaked my friend out at the audition . . .

HAKIJA: Why did you make a joke about what happened to you?

JEN: When? Oh, th[e other]—? I don't know. Because it's sad.

HAKIJA: It's not sad.

JEN: No?

HAKIJA: It's tragic.

JEN: Oh, well—I knew who he was, but I was making a bargain with myself: I thought we could have a beautiful life and he'd make a lot of money and our children would be safe, life would be easy, but I wasn't, I mean, I don't think I was a victim. What? . . . And killing your father and fucking your mother is tragic, my story is . . . What's that [smile]?

HAKIJA: Americans. You all think . . . mortal creatures can win.

JEN: Well—

HAKIJA: An amazing ability.

JEN: Not . . . *all* Americans . . .

HAKIJA: In my experience. You are—more than you think, *yes* . . . much more . . . like our Oedipus:

JEN: How?

HAKIJA: Blind to your own tragedy, not to mention . . .

JEN: Well . . . Maybe so. Mention?

HAKIJA: . . . Anyone else's.

JEN: Right. *(Pause)* Well . . . so . . . were you trying to be funny at the audition when you told that story to Fanny?

HAKIJA: Anything anyone says to someone named Fanny should be funny, don't you think?

JEN: Were you?

HAKIJA: Your friend asked me if there wasn't "like a sort of a war going on" in my country.

JEN: Uh-huh? Well . . . You must be used to that by now? I don't know, I'm only making conversation, / that's—

HAKIJA: No. Not to put too fine a point on it—or risk bringing anyone down—but two hundred thousand of my countrymen, including all of my family, were slaughtered in full view of the world. Our Christian neighbors, who have known us since childhood, for generations—and mind you, these are not peasants, poor people, these are doctors and successful businessmen and lawyers and scientists, my father was a professor of philosophy, *indistinguishable* from you or me if you were to see them—which you couldn't or refused to,

41

I won't speak for you, Americans refused—these people, friends, colleagues, simply because they had Serbian ancestry and we were Muslims, came into our homes, murdered many of the men, raped the women and drove the survivors into camps where most starved to death. That is not, nowhere near the worst. If I were to tell you the worst of what I saw, you would say I was inventing it. Not possible.

JEN: I'm sorry.

HAKIJA: The only people in the world capable of putting a stop to any of this left an embargo on all weapons to one side, ours, and stood by, using so-called humanitarian efforts to excuse themselves from doing anything.

JEN: I'm as ignorant as—

HAKIJA: Of course. You're, as I said, interested in winning. If we agree, *together,* not to see something, then ... Well. And just to be perfectly clear: an American is what I want very much to become; it is only because of American relief efforts, private—

JEN: Yes.

HAKIJA: I am alive at all. So. You mustn't give it another thought. I'll apologize to your ... Fanny.

JEN: No ... I ...

HAKIJA: That was a joke.

JEN: Oh. / Yes.

PAOLA: Okay, we're back.

HAKIJA:
To the blind! May we all be so lucky.
...

PAOLA:
*Here.*

CHRISTMAS:
"They are your troubles, not mine."

NATHANIEL:
Where we left off? Top of whatever the fucking *fuck* ...

HAKIJA:
"For godsakes tell us what you know, we're on our knees to you!"

FANNY *(To Jen):*
Getting acquainted?

NATHANIEL: Shh!

HAKIJA: "You would betray us, keep this knowledge hidden?"

CHRISTMAS: "Time the all-seeing will / find you out again[st your will]!"

HAKIJA: "What is your secret?"

CHRISTMAS: Sorry, sorry, uhhhh,
"You are the murderer of the king,
You are the enemy you seek.
You live in filthy shame with your loved ones."

HAKIJA:

| "Do you begin | CHRISTMAS: |
|---|---|
| to imagine that you | "You are a pathetic wretch to use |
| will ever | these words that soon upon, that |
| escape me? | soon will rain on you!" |

Your life is darkness,
You cannot hurt me or any man
who sees the light."

CHRISTMAS: "/ It is you—"

HAKIJA: "NO MORE! Did Creon put you up to this?
How much? How much did he pay you, stinking *old man*?!?
When the Sphinx held your countrymen in chains, did you speak?
Did you have the answers then?
How convenient you can see the gods' truths now.
Putrefying in your last sick days,
Take your money, take your shame,
Go back to Creon and bow down to him,
On the floor, on your knees,
Serve him however you can,
The two of you in foulest damnest blindness,
I answered her, I stopped the Sphinx, not you,
WHERE WERE YOU THEN?
With my wit, my brains alone,
With *thinking*, not magic! I did it!

I rid this land of that riddling bitch!
With no powers but my own,
Did you witness that?
You claim Apollo on your side,
Run to him now, beg Apollo to save you,
I'll show you what you gain by this treason,
I'll show you things you can't imagine
I'll do it, Oedipus the King!"
CHRISTMAS: "The Tyrant! Not King, Tyrant!"
PAOLA AND FANNY: "Stop, you both speak in anger."
CHRISTMAS: "Pour your hatred on me—" Did I hit you? "—the fates
shall grind you down to nothing, fool!"
NATHANIEL: Okay, okay, that's ... *Good Christ.*
FANNY: Scary.
PAOLA: Loud. Kidding. It was great.
JEN: It really—
NATHANIEL: Okay—
CHRISTMAS: Gee, thanks. Hehe.


## SCENE 7

*Lunch. All but Nathaniel.*

CHRISTMAS: So does Nate have, do you think, like a concept that
Oedipus relates to something more ... current, do you think?
PAOLA: More—? I think—Well, first of all, you should ask him. But
I suspect he'll say he wants the play to speak for itself.

| CHRISTMAS: | FANNY: |
|---|---|
| But I mean like, yeah, but, like ... | I— |
| sometimes I can't tell if he's ... | I— |
| but— | ... |
| Go ahead. | No. You. |
| ... | |

CHRISTMAS *(cont.)*:
Is there a point?, a particular point
of view on the play? We should all ...?

PAOLA: Well, I think he's kind of traditional, but I don't want to
speak for him.

JEN: But if Oedipus is America? Say. *(To Hakija)* Do you want
to ...? And the Chorus is the ongoing debate among the
populace about what's the best course of action like we used
to have before TV made everything one big opinion, annnnd
Jocasta is the conservative because she doesn't want Oedipus to ask any more questions ... This isn't my idea really.

FANNY: Whose is it?

JEN: Do ...?

FANNY: Idea?

JEN: Paola?

FANNY: Hello?

PAOLA: Oh, I hadn't thought about any of that, frankly, I'm still ...

FANNY: I'd just like to / know if—

JEN: We heard.

FANNY: I'm asking about something else now.

JEN: Oh. Sorry.

FANNY: If you and I are one voice or our own voices.

PAOLA: I agree. Let's try it both ways.

JEN: But the idea of responsibility, refusing to accept any—

CHRISTMAS: Yes.

JEN: —blaming everyone else, striking out, ridiculing, isolating
them, insinuating, metaphorically or even literally killing
them and never stopping to ask: What about me? What have
I done? What am I doing to make things worse?

CHRISTMAS: If Oedipus is America and the Chorus is the voting
populace, say, and Jocasta is the, whatever, right of center
sort of—

HAKIJA: Reactionary.

CHRISTMAS: Then Teiresias ...?

HAKIJA: Sees the truth. The petty egos involved.

JEN: Yes.

HAKIJA: He sees through all the lies and knows who is to blame. And says so. These people are always dismissed or jailed, in wartime or any crisis it is not allowed for anyone to say no, to disagree.

JEN AND CHRISTMAS: Right.

HAKIJA: They become traitors.

JEN AND CHRISTMAS: Right.

HAKIJA: Laws are written to silence them; they become more hated than the enemy; and when the war is over everyone agrees to forget what was done to them and who did it.

JEN AND CHRISTMAS: Yes.

FANNY: You two should do Greek Chorus work.

## SCENE 8

*Rehearsal, in medias res.*

FANNY:

| "Jocasta | JEN: |
| enters." Oh, okay, sorry. | *"STOP!"* |

CHRISTMAS: "You'll learn so many things: your true parents, your true acts.

You shall see who you are, with you *(Meant to say "with who," and realizes he misspoke)* you in, *live with*, and in what horror!"

FANNY AND PAOLA: "Who is the / man who—?"

CHRISTMAS: Nate?

NATHANIEL: Yes.

CHRISTMAS: Sorry. We were talking at lunch? About what this, how this, you know, might be something we could connect

to in relation to now? Or how to . . . Anyway, do you think
that Teiresias is like . . . say a kind of left wing, or dissident—

NATHANIEL: No, no, no, no, please don't go there, please don't,
let's not do that, okay, can we just agree we're going to not
try to make the fucking play *relevant* as if it isn't already. Let
people, I mean, give them the courtesy and respect of letting
*them* make those connections.

CHRISTMAS: Oh, okay, yeah, I—

NATHANIEL: Fate requires Oedipus to kill his father and his
mother, and he tries to escape that fate, Teiresias reminds
him that he cannot, he still goes into total denial mode, and
he destroys himself. Left-wing dissident. I love you, come
here. You are very precious. If anything, Teiresias is the *Wall
Street Journal* telling everybody what is completely obvious
if they would get their heads out of their buttholes: America
is fated to be an Empire. That's our true fate.

PAOLA: Pretend you're on the Riviera. / I do.

NATHANIEL: We got all the natural resources, we have the money
and the military might and anybody who pretends that
doesn't come with tremendous responsibilities and prob-
lems is a moron. If we were really smart, we would just blow
up anybody who doesn't get that.

PAOLA: Look at all the pretty bathing suits!

NATHANIEL: Even if it is our fate, we still have to choose it, it isn't
predetermined, you see?

CHRISTMAS: No.

NATHANIEL: You are by far the cutest Teiresias in theater history,
I would concentrate on that.

CHRISTMAS: Okay. I will.

NATHANIEL: Father Christmas, let's start with line . . . oh, what's
the goddamn, "suffering" what is it? "Cause of . . . ?"

HAKIJA: "He says I am the cause of all our suffering!"

NATHANIEL: Thank you.

JEN: "He knows this first hand or he was told?"

HAKIJA: "He claims he speaks for Apollo."

JEN: "Forget these ideas, and hear me out, learn, Oedipus, for
I can teach you something from my experience:
No prophecies are real. I'll prove it.

Once, long ago, an oracle claiming to speak for the gods told
Laius that someday he would die at the hands of his very
own son, our son, and that our child would marry me, bear-
ing sons from a son.

But our son did not live."

HAKIJA: "*You had a son?*"

JEN: "One. At three days old his ankles pierced, *pinned*, crippling
him,
And left upon a barren hill far away from here.
The prophecy is unfulfilled, can't you see?"

NATHANIEL: "Can't *you* see?"

JEN: Oh. "Can't *you* see?"

NATHANIEL: No, no—It's *for* him, it's *to* him—

JEN: Oh, oh.

NATHANIEL: —now don't make it all about yourself—

JEN: Right, right.

NATHANIEL: —forget your feelings—

JEN: Yes.

NATHANIEL: —achieve your actions, / play them.

JEN: Good. I—yes.


"Laius was killed by strangers, not a son, at some place where
three roads meet.
Leave these fears behind—what's wrong?
The gods do what they will, not what these oracles predict."

HAKIJA: "Three roads, you say, that meet? In what country, where?"

JEN: "W—in Phocia."

HAKIJA: "How long ago?"

JEN: "What's wrong?"

HAKIJA: "How long, woman?"

JEN: "Just, uh, well, just before you . . ."

HAKIJA: *"BEFORE?!?!?!"*

JEN:

| | |
|---|---|
| "You came to us. Don't frighten me. What? What is it?" | HAKIJA: "Oh Zeus, what will you have of me?" |
| HAKIJA: "Nothing. Tell me of Laius— How tall, how old, hurry up!" . . . . . . "I've cursed myself!" | JEN: "What of . . . ? Tall, his hair going gray, like yours, his build, not at all unlike yours." |

JEN: "What?"

NATHANIEL: Ask him.

| | |
|---|---|
| HAKIJA: "I've, what, are you deaf?" | JEN: *"What?"* |

HAKIJA: "Who brought the news, how did you learn of his death?!"

JEN: "One servant who escaped alone, but stop, please, you're frightening—"

HAKIJA: "Where is he now?"

JEN: "He saw you on the throne, he ran, what does all this mean?"

HAKIJA: "Nothing, I told you."

JEN: "Nothing? He, he touched my sleeve and begged me send him out into some far-off pasture, far from here."

HAKIJA: "We must see him, have him back."

JEN: "But why?"

HAKIJA: "I fear I have said too much."

JEN: "To your own wife?"

HAKIJA: "Fetch him, fetch him now!"

JEN: "This does not seem like nothing!"

| | |
|---|---|
| HAKIJA: "I won't believe it so until I see: the wickedness within, I won't see it, | JEN: "Believe what?" |

HAKIJA *(cont.)*:
won't call it by a name till it stands there naked and
exposed . . . otherwise, it does not exist. *Go!*"
JEN: "If this be nothing, may I never know a thing." Better?
NATHANIEL: . . . We'll get there.


## SCENE 9

*A bar. All six.*


PAOLA: Why would someone—no, no, hear me out—someone
who'd been warned specifically that he was going to kill his
father and marry his mother ever kill anyone or marry anyone, at all?!, do you see what I'm saying? You're / just *asking*
for trouble.

CHRISTMAS: But he—he thinks he knows his parents, / but he
doesn't.

PAOLA: Yessssss, but still, if you wanted, you see, he's *rash* / —he's
a rash person—

NATHANIEL: That's not his flaw, rashness, plus it's not a flaw in
the sense of character failing. The whole idea of tragic "flaw"
is crap.

CHRISTMAS: Really?

NATHANIEL: Plus— Yes! And it's not about guilt, no one is being
punished—

CHRISTMAS: But—

PAOLA: The tragic "flaw" is no more than an error in judg—

| JEN: | PAOLA: |
|------|--------|
| **What is *wrong*?** | —ment, a foolish act, Oedipus pronouncing the curse on himself, |
| FANNY: | and/or thinking he knows who his |
| **Nothing.** | real parents are. |

JEN:
**Stop it.**
**It's not what**
**you think.**
**You should**
**talk to him.**

FANNY:
**No thank you.**

JEN:
**Why?**

FANNY:
**Because I think**
**he's scary.**
**Not. A nice. Person.**

JEN:
**He's been through an awful**
**lot.**

FANNY:
**He says.**

JEN:
**What does that . . . ?**

FANNY:
**I can** *say* **I'm a ballerina,**
**it doesn't mean I am. Go.**
**Enjoy him.** Maybe he'll tell
you an interesting story.

JEN:
I wish—

CHRISTMAS:
And his pride.

NATHANIEL:
No!

CHRISTMAS:
No?

PAOLA:
Pride was not a sin in
ancient Greece.

CHRISTMAS:
No?

NATHANIEL:
No.

NATHANIEL:
Not at all. Pride was a virtue.
Hubris was a sin.

PAOLA:
Or hybris.

CHRISTMAS:
What's the difference?

NATHANIEL:
Madame?

PAOLA:
Hybris is, means literally water
overflowing its bounds, but it
means figuratively **to treat the**
**less powerful, the weak,**
**unfairly, to bully them, beat**
**them down the way Oedipus**
**speaks to Tereisias**
**and the**

PAOLA:
Well, no.

PAOLA:
No.

FANNY:
I'm not your
mother, it's fine.

PAOLA *(cont.)*:
**Messenger and the
Herdsman, but—**

CHRISTMAS: That's hubris?

FANNY: Trust your instincts. Deeply *flawed* / as they are.

CHRISTMAS: Did you all know that hubris is not pride? It's bullying the weak and powerless! Why don't they teach you that?

JEN: Why don't they teach you that Columbus didn't discover America and was a genocidal maniac?

NATHANIEL: Oh, yes, and you'd be where doing what now if we'd said, "Oh, sorry, Mr. Indian, it's your country, bye, we'll go back to England and be burned at the stake / for having different religious beliefs?"

PAOLA: Oh, please, don't even listen to him . . .

NATHANIEL: "Enjoy!"

JEN:
**So wait. You think our good
fortune now justifies that
slaughter of an entire
civilization?**

PAOLA:
Okay: a drunk
tells him that Polybus and
Merope are not his real
parents and Oedipus
runs to the oracle to
find out the truth—

CHRISTMAS: Right.

NATHANIEL: Yep.

PAOLA: / And the oracle tells him he's going to kill his dad and marry his mom, *but—*

JEN: A whole continent.

NATHANIEL: I'm happy. I didn't have to do it. Fuck 'em.

JEN: Oh, yeah, well. Good, great.

PAOLA: I promise you he's only trying to see how deep your capacity for disgust goes. San Tropez!

HAKIJA *(To Jen)*: You okay?

PAOLA:
*(To Christmas)*
But since
this isn't
what he wanted
to hear or
asked about
he totally
ignores the
earlier information
that his real
parents might be
elsewhere and
races away from
his adopted
parents so he
won't kill and
fuck *them*,
then kills the
very first man
he meets in
Thebes and
marries the
very first
woman he meets
whose husband,
by the way, has
suddenly
disappeared and
has most likely
been killed.

FANNY:
So Nate?

JEN:
**Oh yeah. I'm starting to see your
point about Americans. Some anyway.**

HAKIJA:
**Yes?**

JEN:
**Nate—Never mind.
And Fanny . . . [who] doesn't like
me talking to you.**

HAKIJA:
**No?**

JEN:
**No. She thinks you're dangerous.**

HAKIJA:
**Oh, well, I am. Very. I am the
plague, remember?**

JEN:
**How are you doing—with . . . ?**

HAKIJA:
**Okay. I guess. I'm learning a lot.**

JEN:
**Oh good.
Yes?**

HAKIJA:
**I don't know. You tell me.**

JEN:
**He likes you. He has a lot of
credits. Too. I mean,
he's done a lot.**

HAKIJA:
**Yes?**

JEN:
I saw his bio.
It's . . . pretty
impressive.

HAKIJA:
Yes? . . .
Good for him.

JEN:
**So . . .**

NATHANIEL:
**Hak? . . . Hak? You know
I think you're the farthest
thing from that.
You're going to make
me look like Elia-
fucking-Kazan.**

HAKIJA:
**Who's that?**

PAOLA:
I mean, he isn't
acting in any way
reasonably, he's acting
crazy and telling
himself he's being
rational, you
see?

NATHANIEL:
**Who are you arguing with?**

PAOLA:
**I'm not arguing—Don't— / I'm
only—**

NATHANIEL:
**I know, just, just / checking.**

PAOLA:
It's the most modern thing about the play:
What human beings don't want to know,
they just literally allow themselves not to know.

CHRISTMAS:
That is so cool. I never would have
thought of that.

PAOLA:
Can I scooch in here?
Here's what I'm saying:
He's born to one set
of parents,
abandoned on a hillside
with his feet pinned
together, **he's even
named for it:**

NATHANIEL:
Ouch. Straight to the
the nursing home for me.
**Listen, I'll introduce you
to any casting agent,
producer, director,** whatever
you want, New York, LA,
just say the word.
**You may think I'm
just some backwater
*hack*, but I'm serious.**
HAKIJA:
**Thank you.**
JEN: **Wow.**

NATHANIEL:
**You take me up on it,
all right?**

HAKIJA:
**All right.**

FANNY:
**Nate?**
NATHANIEL:
**Mm?**

JEN:
**That was pretty great.**

Listen. I want to ask you

PAOLA *(cont.)*:
**Oieden pous,
"Swell Foot."**
But he doesn't even
ask himself why
he's named that, or
why he limps!
It would be as if my
**name were Paola, Dumped
in the Sea!
You think I'd be
sort of curious.**
CHRISTMAS:
**Pretty name, though.**
PAOLA:
But: no curiosity!
All he has to do
is stop and add
up the clues.

CHRISTMAS:
But—but he still couldn't
stop it from—
because of fate.
Right?
PAOLA:
You know, let it go:
We're all **fated.**
You're **fated** to
be tall, funny, long-
lived, **you're fated to be gay.**
CHRISTMAS:
**You can tell?**              FANNY:
                              Nate?

55

JEN *(cont.)*:
something. From . . .
What makes neighbors
and friends, colleagues
. . . you don't have
to talk about this if—

HAKIJA:
Go ahead, no.

JEN:
Well . . .

. . .

. . .

. . .

Do those things.
You said.

HAKIJA:
Greed. It isn't complicated.
The Serbs got rich off the
slaughter and removal of
Muslims. Our land and
houses, jobs—Milosevic
built himself a
palace, many shiny new
limousines in Beograd.

JEN:
I see.

HAKIJA:
They use religion,
nationalism—

PAOLA:
No, I just assumed.
Not because you're
femmy or anything,
it's the way
you look at people
according to gender.

CHRISTMAS:
But . . . can I ask:
Am I really fake
as the Messenger?

PAOLA:
Not to me.
. . .
Why do you
think you feel
that?

CHRISTMAS:
Oh, it's just . . .
I guess the
size of it.

PAOLA:
Yes.

FANNY *(cont.)*:
I'm curious:
What
made you
decide to
stay in
Cambridge
rather than
starting a
company in,
I don't know,
New
York or
in some
other city, it
seems
like this town—

NATHANIEL:
Oh, we
really like it here.
I love it
actually.

FANNY:
Uh-huh.

NATHANIEL:
We were both
sick of New
York, the LA
rat race, we
thought it would
be better for

JEN:
Yes.

HAKIJA:
—to justify their acts.

...

Very smart.

...

Play to people's fear.
Tell Serbs we Muslims
want them dead. And
of course always there
is a crazy person in any
group, even Muslims,
saying crazy things, you
can point to that one.

HAKIJA:
No one of us believed
our good
friends could do
these things.

...

But...

JEN:
They could...

CHRISTMAS:
The heightened
language.

PAOLA:
How have you
and Nate been
approaching it?

CHRISTMAS:
The Messenger?

PAOLA:
Don't tell him I
asked you—

CHRISTMAS:
Of course
not.

PAOLA:
I don't want to
interfere with
your process, or
his.

CHRISTMAS:
Well he feels, or
says that I have to
find a way, like,

NATHANIEL *(cont.)*:
our health,
we got out of
the constant
looking [for], the
competition—
let our union
memberships
expire.

FANNY:
Sure. You
should have
signed them
over to me.
...Go on.

NATHANIEL:
It's liberating
to start over.
Reinvent
yourself. Start
again.

NATHANIEL:
It is. And very
few people get
to have that.
Without

CRAIG LUCAS

JEN *(cont.)*:
...
...
**Have you read Marx?**

HAKIJA:
**Oh, he is required reading for me.**

JEN:
**As an actor? Cool.**

HAKIJA: **No, I am economics major.**

JEN:
You are?

But you've studied acting.

*(Hakija shakes his head no.)*

**Yes you have.**

HAKIJA:
**I am a very bad liar, trust me.**

JEN:
**I'm really dumbstruck. Do you know how good you are?**
...

CHRISTMAS *(cont.)*:
a need to unburden myself or something, that it's a life-threatening trauma this guy faces because of what he sees, but it's really hard to find—I don't know . . .

PAOLA:
What if . . . you know **how when you** witness something historic, I mean, in person, or you see someone being interviewed.

CHRISTMAS:
**Right.**

PAOLA:
**Being right there when John Hinkley shot— or that crazy man who killed John Lennon—**
...
**It's weird the** way humans react to violence and **suffering.**

CHRISTMAS:
**What do you mean? W—?**

NATHANIEL *(cont.)*:
**destroying themselves.**
...
I mean—

FANNY:
Yeah.

NATHANIEL:
I'm quite—I **believe that—** I'm not being coy and ironic. *(Nathaniel explains his directorial ethos to Fanny\*)*

* See Appendix B for the rest of this speech, page 121.

JEN *(cont.)*:
**Well, I do.**
**For whatever it's worth.**

...

...

I'm so glad to finally talk to
somebody about, I don't know,
ideas. I'd ... I mean, if this
subject is too difficult.

HAKIJA:
**My life, you mean.**

JEN:
**Well, the world, all of us.**
**Why does everyone keep**
**moving away, do I smell?**

HAKIJA:
**Yes.**

JEN:
**I do?**

HAKIJA:
**You smell good.**
**Go on.**

JEN:
**Oh ...**

...

...

**Well ... okay:**
**Do you hate them? The**
**Serbs? You must.**

*(Hakija finds a book.)*

PAOLA:
**People love it! Suffering! Pain!**
**Cruelty. They love to watch it,**
**not to endure it, but**
**see it. It's gratifying to see**
**people in agony *if* you're in a**
**safe enough spot on the side-**
**lines, movies, TV, *tragedy*, of**
**course. Somebody tells you about**
**something awful, the TV news,**
**talk about suffering, the entire**
***world*, why do we look at it?**

CHRISTMAS:
**Yes!**

PAOLA:
**Well, that's what I'm saying**
**about the Messenger.**
He's got a story to tell: a lot
of bad news. He knows that
everyone is listening, carefully.

CHRISTMAS:
**This is very helpful.**

PAOLA:
**Well, as long as it doesn't**
**interfere with what Nate's**
**doing and what he wants.**

CHRISTMAS:
**I understand.**

PAOLA:
**Important question: Do you
sleep with women too?**

HAKIJA:
I found this when I was
preparing for my audition.
From *Ajax*:
"Our enemies must be
despised as ones who
will someday become
our friends, and our
**friends must be
helped, always, as
ones who may not
always be friends.**
...
**For most men the
safety of—"**

CHRISTMAS:
What is this, first
rehearsal, should I
**strip or something?**

*(Fanny listens
to the Paola/
Christmas
conversation.)*

PAOLA:
**Sure.**

CHRISTMAS:
I...
...
...
...
**Sometimes, I do.**

FANNY:
How many women?
In your whole life.

JEN AND HAKIJA:
**"—friendship, of
love, will  not last."**

CHRISTMAS:
**Women?**
...
...
**Let's see ...**
...
...
**One.**

HAKIJA:
**You know it?**

JEN:
**A lot of students do it for class.**
...

JEN *(cont.)*:
**"Everything is brought by time
itself from—"**
JEN AND HAKIJA:
"—darkness into light."

*(Hakija does something slightly
intimate to Jen: touching her hand
or rubbing his temple against
hers. She allows this to go on, but
turns her attention to whatever is
being said by the others. Hakija
will slowly venture more surreptitiously
to Jen's hand under the table, her
knee, her thigh, finally moving his
hand up her thigh and directly
onto her nether regions.)*

CHRISTMAS *(cont.)*:
. . .
. . .
**And a half.**
FANNY:
Ooo, what was that
like?
**The half?**
*(To Nathaniel)*
**Sorry.**

*(If Nathaniel still has more
of his directing credo to go,
he can finish now. If not:)*

NATHANIEL:
**I've finished grinding
my ax.**

FANNY: Why don't you go Equity, though?

NATHANIEL: Oh, A.R.T. is in town, you know.

PAOLA: Oh, Nate, for heaven's sake.

NATHANIEL: What?

PAOLA: These are our friends.

NATHANIEL: Okay, it's not up to me.

PAOLA: I have HIV, and I'm doing fine, really well, but for a time
I wasn't and we stopped everything, and we're only finally
just getting ourselves out of hibernation.

FANNY: Wow.

PAOLA: I hate making any fuss about it, it's been so many years,
the less I talk about it the better for me, frankly, so . . . but
this is our inaugural production.

FANNY: Oh, cool.

PAOLA: [Very first.] Yes, so . . . / We're very excited about it. We
really are.

*(Over the end of this Jen suddenly pulls away from Hakija.)*

JEN: Stop, god . . . [What is wrong with you?] I'm sorry, it's not you, I'm . . . it's me, I just . . . I have to learn lines, I have to go, it's . . . Really—Sorry everybody.

*(Hakija is mortified. Jen is pleading to Fanny with her eyes: "Get me out of here!")*

FANNY: Welp, I'm out too, then.

CHRISTMAS: Ohhhhhh.

PAOLA: I'll drop you.

CHRISTMAS: We just got here!

PAOLA: It's late.

NATHANIEL: Okay.

PAOLA: You don't have to for me.

NATHANIEL: We have a big day tomorrow. Another night. Okay?

CHRISTMAS: You going too?

HAKIJA: One / more.

| PAOLA: | JEN: |
|---|---|
| Good night everyone. | Wait up! |
| NATHANIEL: | FANNY: |
| Night. | I'm not going anywhere. |
| Good work everybody. | |
| See you in the morning. | |

Unless you all want to come up to our place.

PAOLA: If you're going to stay up—

NATHANIEL: / Oh, right—All right.

PAOLA: That was the point of my leaving.

NATHANIEL: Yes / yes.

PAOLA: I want to sleep.

NATHANIEL: Of course.

PAOLA: It's fine.

NATHANIEL: No, no, we should. Sleep. G'night.

*(All exit but Hakija and Christmas. Pause.)*

CHRISTMAS: That was weird. *(Short pause)* What happened? What do you think? Did something . . . I thought everybody was having a good time. *(Pause)* What did it . . . What did it seem like to you? *(Pause)* Those two.

HAKIJA: Fear.

CHRISTMAS: Fear?

HAKIJA: That's what it seemed like.

CHRISTMAS: Of? . . . That you would . . . talk about things in Yugo-slavia, maybe? Or . . .

HAKIJA: Just fear.

CHRISTMAS: Oh. Fear . . . Of . . .

HAKIJA: Just . . .

CHRISTMAS: Oh. But . . . Okay. Fear of what though? Sex? Or . . . ? *(Pause)* Oh, I see, if you say what kind then it's not *just* fear. *(Pause)* So . . . *(Pause)* Fear. *(Pause)* You . . . think she's hot? Jen. *(Short pause)* What? Okay, mystery, right. Okay. Forgot. *(Silence)* To mystery. And . . . fear. *(Short pause)* And pity. *(Silence)* Terror and pity. *(Pause)* So what was it like? . . . The war?

# ACT TWO

## SCENE 1

JEN *(To us; holding up Hakija's book)*: *Ajax*:
>Everything is brought by time itself
>From darkness into light
>Then consigned once more to night,
>Nothing so catastrophic
>That man can trust it never to come to pass,
>No promise, nor force of will,
>No edifice so fierce, so high,
>It cannot come down upon our heads.
>We must learn to yield to the gods.

I don't believe that.

## SCENE 2

*Rehearsal. All six.*

PAOLA: "Haughtiness,"
FANNY: "pride,"
PAOLA AND FANNY: "and"
PAOLA: "violence"
FANNY: "breed"
PAOLA AND FANNY: "tyranny; the"
PAOLA: "Tyrant"
FANNY: "/ means to—"
PAOLA: / May [I]?
NATHANIEL: Keep going, please.
PAOLA: "cli / mb"
FANNY: "climb to"
PAOLA AND FANNY: "heights"
PAOLA: "belonging to the"
PAOLA AND FANNY: "gods."
FANNY: "May the"
PAOLA AND FANNY: "gods"
PAOLA: "bring him to"
PAOLA AND FANNY: "ruin,"
FANNY: "cast him"
PAOLA AND FANNY: "down,"
PAOLA: "tear him"
PAOLA AND FANNY: "apart,"
FANNY: "reward his"
PAOLA AND FANNY: "hubris—"
NATHANIEL: *People.*
FANNY: "—with—" Go on?
NATHANIEL: Please.
FANNY: "with"

PAOLA: "no"

PAOLA AND FANNY: "profit"

PAOLA: "whatsoever: break the"

PAOLA AND FANNY: "Tyrant's neck—"

FANNY: That's just me. "—neck. Make him"

PAOLA AND FANNY: "untouchable."

PAOLA: "If the"

PAOLA AND FANNY: "gods"

FANNY: "allow the"

PAOLA AND FANNY: "Tyrant"

PAOLA: "to go"

PAOLA AND FANNY: "free"

FANNY: "/ I re[fuse]—"

NATHANIEL: It won't be as funny when strangers have paid money and you look completely bereft of talent.

FANNY: "I—" / Haha—

PAOLA: "refuse / to celebrate in their honor."

FANNY *(Catching up)*: "refuse to celebrate in their honor." Ooo, that was kind of cool.

PAOLA: When are we / allowed to ask questions?

NATHANIEL: Yes? Yes, ask, now, please, perfect timing.

PAOLA: First of all—well, why did you change it from "dance" to "celebrate."

NATHANIEL: You tell me.

FANNY: *You tell me.*

NATHANIEL: Fanny.

FANNY: Because we're not dancing.

NATHANIEL: That would be one reason.

PAOLA: But it's a *famous*, famous line, "The Chorus sang and danced, in dialect no less—"

NATHANIEL: I'm per—

PAOLA: —and now they are saying, "We won't dance anymore if this whole thing—this whole Dionysian theatrical annual celebration is for naught."

NATHANIEL: Yes?

PAOLA: Well—

NATHANIEL: Your other question?

PAOLA: If we're not going to— Oh never mind.

NATHANIEL: Go on.

PAOLA: I forget now— Oh. Breaking it up that way creates a kind of expectedness—

NATHANIEL: That's right.

PAOLA: —that could be construed as kind of—

NATHANIEL: Of?

PAOLA: Unintentionally—

NATHANIEL: Comic? Only if we do it badly.

PAOLA: Oh, I see, the onus is entirely on us, then.

NATHANIEL: That's correct.

PAOLA: Well, if this onus is entirely on me, then I'm—us—

FANNY: Thank you.

PAOLA: I'm going to ask the unaskable.

NATHANIEL: Shoot.

PAOLA: Why are there only two of us? Two Elders? In all of Thebes. It has to mean something if we're going to do that. I mean, is everyone else is dead from the plague?

NATHANIEL: Okay.

PAOLA: No, not okay: What are you intending? Why two?

NATHANIEL: Fanny?

FANNY: Beeeeecause the director is a sadist?

NATHANIEL: Why else?

FANNY: Beeeecause you want us to find a way to represent many people?

NATHANIEL: Go on.

FANNY: Beeeeeecause the Elders are of two minds at all times, their thoughts go back and forth.

NATHANIEL: Okay.

PAOLA: Then it isn't broken up properly.

NATHANIEL: Then break it up another way.

PAOLA: Don't be that way.

NATHANIEL: I'm not being—

FANNY: Okay, we will.

NATHANIEL: Okay, until we receive that, let's take it from the second stasimon: "Fate moves . . ." whatever the / bloody hell—

FANNY: Is that true they sang and danced these in dialect?

PAOLA: In masks and fancy shoes. It would be as if we performed with Appalachian accents and ukuleles.

FANNY: In high heels. / Basic[ally]—

NATHANIEL: "For fate moves swift."

PAOLA: And it's an ode, not a stasimon.

| JEN: | FANNY: |
|---|---|
| *(To Christmas)* **Hey.** *(Pause)* **You okay?** | "Whoever committed this bloody crime had better fly from here for" |
| . . . | PAOLA AND FANNY:<br>"*fate* moves swift" |
| | FANNY:<br>"with" |
| **What's up?** | |
| | PAOLA AND FANNY: |
| *(Pause.)* | "fire" |
| | FANNY: |
| **You guys stay late?** | "and" |
| | PAOLA AND FANNY: |
| *(Pause.)* | "light." |
| JEN: | FANNY: |
| **Christmas?** | "I don't know what to think— |
| . . . | Oedipus? The killer?" |
| CHRISTMAS: | PAOLA: |
| **He told me horrible things.** | "What motive would he have?" |
| JEN: | FANNY: |
| **Hak? . . . Like? . . .** | "I would never find fault with our Tyrant who saved the city, banished |

CHRISTMAS:
**It's kind of . . .**

JEN:
**You don't have
to tell me.**
CHRISTMAS:
**No, it's really
upsetting . . .**
JEN:
**Oh. Well . . .**

**. . .**

**If . . .**
CHRISTMAS:
**He saw
his whole
family
murdered.
He was the
only one
of the
whole
village to
survive.
His mother
was shot
in the back,
right in front
of him. They
made his
father and**

FANNY *(cont.)*:
the Sphinx. Never will I condemn
him."

PAOLA:
Before—I'm sorry—before . . . Nate?
You use Tyrant to mean what it
means to us, and now you use it as the
Greeks meant it.
NATHANIEL:
/ Yes.
FANNY:
What—? / I'm—

PAOLA:
Well, how is the audience to—?
NATHANIEL:
They're *kelp*, no matter how much
you explain, how clear you are, they
will still be kelp.
FANNY:
I don't understand what it meant to
the Greeks.

NATHANIEL:
/ Someone not born king.

PAOLA:
A king who is—yes, chosen.

FANNY:
And what is kelp, why kelp?

CHRISTMAS *(cont.)*:
**brother dance**
**on the edge**
**of a bridge**
**and stuffed**
**pork in their**
**mouths and**
**then pushed**
**them over**
**the edge.**
*(Pause)*
**Their**
**heads**
**washed**
**up in**
**a trash**
**bag down**
**the river**
**in another**
**town. I**
**mean,**
**who would,**
**what kind**
**of person**
**would**
**tell you**
**that? . . .**
**You know?**
**Your own**
**father?**

NATHANIEL:
Bottom of the ocean, no light, waving
their insensate tendrils: you have to
shine an awfully bright beam down
there to even reach them at all,
god knows what they perceive:
*kelp.* Okay, again from, ummm—
Anywhere.

PAOLA:
"What motive would he have?"

FANNY:
"I would never find fault with
our Tyrant—"

PAOLA:
. . .                                    Me, either.
. . .
"—whoooo saved the city,
banished the Sphinx. Never
will I condemn him."

                                         Me, either.

NATHANIEL:
"Citizens, is this true?
What I hear?

Oedipus has
accused me of                    Oh sure.
conspiring with the
Soothsayer?"

FANNY:
"It is, I fear."

| FANNY *(cont.)*: | PAOLA *(cont.)*: |
|---|---|
| ... | Say, |
| "Here he is now!" | here he is now! |

HAKIJA:
"You! Did you or did you not tell me
to send for that middlesex mumbler,
your little prophet for hire!"
Why middlesex?

NATHANIEL:
Good question. Why middlesexed?

CHRISTMAS: Hm? Me?

NATHANIEL: Why "middlesex"?

CHRISTMAS: I'm sorry, what?

NATHANIEL: Oedipus calls Teiresias "middlesexed." Why?

CHRISTMAS: Beeeeeecause he's overwrought?

NATHANIEL: Why else?

CHRISTMAS: Because he's a homophobe?

NATHANIEL: Do your research. *(To Hakija, voice low)* He's middlesexed—

CHRISTMAS: Oh, you'll tell him, but I have to do my research.

| PAOLA: | |
|---|---|
| Because Seers were often | NATHANIEL: |
| hermaphrodites, that's why. | Go on. |

HAKIJA: "Did you think I would not defend myself?
Did you think me such an imbecile?"

NATHANIEL: "Am I allowed to answer these charges?"

| HAKIJA: | |
|---|---|
| "No! | *(Paola gestures for Fanny* |
| You're too good." | *to follow her to a quiet place.)* |

| | PAOLA: |
|---|---|
| NATHANIEL: | What if we were to ... |
| You're upstaging yourself. | |
| *(To Paola)* SH! | |

NATHANIEL *(cont.)*:
*(To Hakija)* You have your
back to the audience.

CHRISTMAS *(To Jen)*:
**They had camps . . .
whole rape
camps . . . A
friend's sister
was videotaped
being raped . . .
and they . . .
mutilated her
and kept the
camera running.
Killed her.
On tape. He
saw it . . . Who—?
What kind of
a person would
show you that?
. . . They beat
the men with
sledgehammers . . .
to death. In
public . . . They
dragged the,
some professor
he knew, grew
up with,
somebody else
he knew, tied
the guy to the
back of a car and
dragged him**

*(Paola and Fanny move out of sight.)*

HAKIJA:
I don't care.

NATHANIEL:
I do.

HAKIJA:
I can act with
my back, can't
I? We'll see
it on your
face.
*(Returns to play:)*
"When Laius
disappeared, was
your prophet in
business then?"

NATHANIEL:
"Yes, and equally
respected."

HAKIJA:
"Did he mention me then?"

NATHANIEL:
"Not that I'm aware."

HAKIJA:
"Only now he accuses me."

CHRISTMAS *(cont.)*:
**until he was**
**just . . . bones**
**and . . . tendons . . .**
*(Pause)* **It's**
**so horrible.**
*(Pause)*
**People are**
**so horrible.**

JEN:
**It's okay, babe.**

CHRISTMAS:
**Oh . . . Nate is**
**so mean to me.**

*(Pause.)*

JEN:
**. . . Nate?**

CHRISTMAS:
**I'm . . . Oh**
**god . . .**
**I'm so in**
**love with**
**him . . .**
**I'm sorry.**
**I can't . . .**

JEN:
**Shhhhh.**
**Shhhhh.**

CHRISTMAS:
**Go. I'm fine, it's fine.**

NATHANIEL:
"Be reasonable. Do you, my
sister, and I not rule
together? Why would I
risk such foolishness
when I already have the
power anyone might
seek? If you don't
believe me, go to Delphi,
but don't judge me based
on supposition—Take the
time, for time is the great
teacher—" Elders?

PAOLA AND FANNY:
*(Entering together)*
"He speaks wisely: quick
tempers lead to quick ends!"

HAKIJA:
"If I don't move swiftly, I'll
be swiftly undone."

NATHANIEL:
"Do you mean to banish me?"

HAKIJA:
"I mean to kill you, sir."

NATHANIEL:
"Have you lost your mind?"

PAOLA AND FANNY:
**"Stop! Jocasta comes! Listen to**
**to reason!"**

NATHANIEL:
. . . Jo / casta [comes]!

JEN: "You should be ashamed to have this private squabble with the city in despair—
Get inside, both of you!"

NATHANIEL: "Sister, he wants me executed."

HAKIJA: "With good reason."

NATHANIEL: "May the gods take me if I am guilty as charged."

JEN: "Trust him, please, he swears to the gods, for my sake, and all those standing here."

FANNY: I love being a crowd.

HAKIJA: "But he accused me of murdering Laius!"

JEN: "He knew this himself or learned it somehow?"

HAKIJA: "He put the profiteering prophet up to it so he could appear free of guilt."

NATHANIEL:
It's really hard to invest
in anything if you're both
making cracks and whispering.
...
Jen.

FANNY:
Sorry.
...
Sorry.

PAOLA:
Sorry.

JEN: Yeah.

NATHANIEL: It's about him.

JEN: Still.

NATHANIEL: It's always about him.

JEN: No, I—

NATHANIEL: It's always about the other person.

JEN: I understand.

NATHANIEL: Understanding is the booby prize. Stop him, stop Creon, get them inside, don't feel sorry for yourself.

JEN: I wasn't [trying to]—That isn't what I was trying to [play]—

NATHANIEL: If crying were acting, my great-aunt Harriet would be Duse. Okay, let's . . . everything okay?

JEN: He's fine.

NATHANIEL: Okay, your homework . . . Should we break?

CHRISTMAS: No, I'm listening, I'm fine.

NATHANIEL: ... is ... to look into your own lives ...

FANNY: Noooooo!

NATHANIEL: —and to change the narrative, but by only as much as you need to in order to place yourself at the center of a tragedy. A dramatic tragedy, not, "Oh, I got hit by a bus and killed," that's tragic for you and the people who love you ... but not in the sense that we're talking about.

FANNY: What's the diff, Buddha boy? ... You tell me.

CHRISTMAS: ... Me? Oh, fate! Which is not predetermination, oh no!, no no!

NATHANIEL: Fate what?

CHRISTMAS: The gods ... I'm sorry, I didn't get a lot of sleep ... the gods' will or design, I don't know, intersect with the desires of man and man always pays. Right?

NATHANIEL: That's exactly right.

CHRISTMAS: / Really?

FANNY: But, but, you know? Okay: I had the same problem with AA, okay? I don't believe in god. I don't believe in a higher power.

NATHANIEL: No? Who will you pray to for help with your acting?

FANNY: So mean.

NATHANIEL: Anyway, that's your homework. Oh—yes—lest you go seeking some cozy little narrative in which your personal flaws, your procrastination or your inability to quit smoking—your *guilt*, primarily—From—you can ... [read it]. Charles what is his name?

PAOLA: Segal. *(Reads)* "... it is precisely by showing Oedipus's life against its earlier success and power that Sophocles defines it as tragic and thus creates the form of the 'tragic hero' in Western literature: a figure whose force of personality and integrity—"

NATHANIEL: *Integrity.*

PAOLA: "—set him (or her) apart for a special destiny of pain and struggle—"

NATHANIEL: *Special destiny.*

PAOLA: "—and enable him to confront that destiny with clarity
and courage . . . after a difficult journey to self-knowledge."

NATHANIEL: Yes? What would it take, what would you have to
change in order for your story to even deserve to be consid-
ered tragic? *Self-knowledge.* Ah! NOW I SEE! At last. "T'was
blind but now I see." "Time, the—" What the fuck is it?

PAOLA: "Time, the all-seeing, has found you out against your will."

NATHANIEL: "Count no man fortunate till he is dead."

CHRISTMAS: Nice.

NATHANIEL: That's your homework.

FANNY: Time the all-seeing is about to find us out.

NATHANIEL: And this is just for you, I don't want you to tell these.

## SCENE 3

*The bar. All six.*

JEN: **I'm not. I'm not going to sleep with him.**

CHRISTMAS *(To Nathaniel)*: **Movies?!?**

FANNY: **Well, I happen to know** / otherwise.

| | NATHANIEL: |
|---|---|
| JEN: | **The greatest single** |
| **No.** You don't shit where you eat. | **corrupting influence** |
| | **in the twentieth** |
| | **century.** |
| FANNY: | **Look:** |
| Should sex be compared to feces? | **The worst century** |
| | **in the history** |
| JEN: | **of all mankind.** |
| We're working together, it's too soon | **How many** |
| to me to for to sleep with / anyone— | **people were killed by** |
| | **other people—** |

FANNY:
You're drunk.

JEN:
—for me to sleep with anyone, I'm
not, much less get involved.

FANNY:
**But he's so cute.**
JEN:
**I know.**

FANNY:
**I caught you! I don't think he's
cute at all!**

JEN:
**Yes—you do.**

FANNY:
**No! I think he's a user, and if you're
not careful you're going to be helping
him become a citizen and a movie star**
and raising his kids because you think he's
a "winner" so you're hitching your little
wagon to him like you did with Bart, and he
may be a winner, but that isn't going to stop
him from dumping you for another movie
star and then you'll be right where you are
now except with teeny-tiny toddlers, so you
can say goodbye to acting once and for all.
JEN:
**Thank you, Teiresias.**

NATHANIEL *(cont.)*:
**Hundreds of
millions— Stalin,
Hitler, Pol Pot—**
. . .
***What?***
PAOLA:
*(Into Nathaniel's ear)*
You seemed so calm
today. You're not . . . ?
NATHANIEL:
No, I'm not. But
thanks for trusting me.
Milosevic—one long
nightmare . . . And
what do you *know*?!?
When did movies
start? At the top the
top of the self-same
century! Have it:
empirical evidence!

CHRISTMAS:
**But—**

PAOLA:
**Don't even bother—**

CHRISTMAS:
**—couldn't movies be a
symptom of the disease**

*(Pause.)*

JEN:
You think he's going to be a movie star?

FANNY:
I do.

JEN:
Me, too.

FANNY:
A mean movie star.

JEN:
You don't mean any of this.

FANNY:
Now who is it who married the doctor who took all of her hard-earned money and all her years of effort and—

JEN:
Okay, we've covered this.

FANNY:
—who claims to have known deep down what an unscrupulous worm he really was but stayed with him out of some kind of / blind desire to fix or be taken [care]—

CHRISTMAS *(cont.)*:
**rather than the actual / source?**

NATHANIEL:
**No! Because they objectify human beings, they're literally *not* there! They're shadows of people doing things from the past, they can be dead, and often are.**

HAKIJA:
**I like movies.**

NATHANIEL:
**Of course you do. When people are blown to smithereens in movies they're not real. Onstage, the actors are there, live, right in front of you, it's more dangerous, anything could happen, it's the complete antidote to cynicism.**

CHRISTMAS:
**Do you hey do you think that's why the Republicans are always trying to cut funding to the arts?**

NATHANIEL:
**I'm Republican.**

CHRISTMAS:
**Right.**

| JEN: | PAOLA: |
|------|--------|
| Thank you, / thank you very— | **Not out of conviction, just to appall as many people as possible in as few words.** |
| FANNY: | CHRISTMAS: |
| I wash my hands of you. | **Really, though?** |

PAOLA: Look, Cap d'Antibes, *nice!*

CHRISTMAS: If that's true, even if you were to beg me, I would not ever let you ride my face like a mechanical bull. And that decision is final.


## SCENE 4

*Rehearsal. All six. This sequence takes us to opening night.*

CHRISTMAS: "Jocasta's dead: her own hand."

NATHANIEL: Okay. What do you want from them?

CHRISTMAS: Tooooo inform them?

NATHANIEL: That's what you're doing, what do you want / from—

| PAOLA: | FANNY: |
|--------|--------|
| Nate? | We have to show you! |
| NATHANIEL: | |
| We're working. | |
| PAOLA: | Two seconds, sorry, Chris. |
| Take a look at what we— Ready? | . . . |
| Hit it! | And a one two three four! |

*(Paola and Fanny are in sunglasses and high heels, singing a blues version of:)*

PAOLA AND FANNY: "Add up all the men—ever lived and ever died!
Add my poor life to theirs and what do you get?
Nothing!
Nothing!

Has there ever been a man whose joy was more than smoke?
A vision born in chaos
Then blown to hell again!
You! Oedipus! Our shining star!
You were high and mighty.
And happy as a clam!
Priceless fame and glory!
And what did it get you?
Nothing!
(What did it get you?)
Nothing!
(Nothing I say!)
A whole lotta nothing!
YESSIR!
Nothing. No! Thing!"

FANNY: That's as far as we've gotten.

NATHANIEL: What do you want from them? You describe the scene—

CHRISTMAS: Oh, *from* . . .

NATHANIEL: —because youuuuu . . . ?

CHRISTMAS: Ummmm—Tooooo—make them . . . see it?

NATHANIEL: Yes. Okay.

CHRISTMAS: "Jocasta's dead: her own hand.

You weren't there,

you can't—know . . ."

NATHANIEL: Go ahead.

CHRISTMAS: Can . . . ? I was—What if when I start relaying what I saw, I'm actually sort of thrilled deep down to have been witness to this hideous thing.

NATHANIEL: I don't . . .

CHRISTMAS: Well, you know how like when you have really bad news about someone important, it makes you feel important too?

NATHANIEL: Uhhh—

FANNY: Yes! Abso / lutely.

CHRISTMAS: Like . . . um . . . the people who are there when some like when a politician gets shot, killed, if you are there, you take on some of the grandeur or . . . You become more—

FANNY: That is . . . Isn't that true though?

NATHANIEL: It's interesting. I hadn't—

CHRISTMAS: I mean, I know you said he's in shock, really traumatized, but . . .

NATHANIEL: Well, try it.

CHRISTMAS: And that's true, too.

NATHANIEL: Sure. Why not? Give it a—

CHRISTMAS: Yes?

NATHANIEL: Paola?

PAOLA: I'm sorry, I wasn't listening. What?

NATHANIEL: Give it a—

CHRISTMAS: Okay. I mean, if it doesn't work . . .

NATHANIEL: Yes, absolutely.

CHRISTMAS: "I was. I was there.

> She burst in, a queen, our queen,
> Now demented and wringing her hair,
> Running through doors, running—
> Then locks herself in the bedroom, crying:
> 'Laius, here is our bed, soiled.'"

Does—?

NATHANIEL: It's good, keep going.

CHRISTMAS: Oh, good.

FANNY: I love that. Sorry.

CHRISTMAS:

| | |
|---|---|
| "You weren't there. | JEN: |
| You can't know how | **I wish I could have** |
| horrible it was. | **known your family.** |
| I was. I was there. | **. . .** |
| She burst in, a queen, our queen, | **How in the world** |

CHRISTMAS *(cont.)*:
now demented and wringing her hair,
running through doors, running—"

JEN *(cont.)*:
**did such an amazing person
come about?**

NATHANIEL:
Make me see it.

*(Pause. Soon Jen and Hakija
will begin to make out.)*

CHRISTMAS:
"—running, running through doors,
then locks herself in the bedroom,
crying:
'Laius! Here is our bed!
Soiled.
Filthy *soil* bringing forth a husband
by a husband,
And children by a child!
All soiled!
We made love!'
Which we does she mean?
Then the son, husband,
king, prince, raving,
stamping up and down and
bellows:
'**A weapon!**
Now! Where is she?
Find me that double breeding
ground!

**Could I see your town some-
day?**

*(Hakija shakes his head no.)*

**No?**

HAKIJA:
**Not with me.**

JEN:
**You would never go?**

**"All killed save one."**

FANNY:
**Why do you stay with Nate?**

Where?'
And hurls himself against the door,
breaking the bolts,
falling to his knees before:
His . . . wife . . . mother . . .
hanging by the neck, twisted."

PAOLA:
**What a funny question.**

FANNY:
**No, I know you love him,
and he loves you, but . . .**

*(Silence.)*

CHRISTMAS:
**"He frees her from the noose,**
noose, glides her down, removes the
golden pins, fingering them—
Holds them up . . . then rams the
long pins into: 'Wicked, wicked /
eyes!'"
NATHANIEL:
**It's scarier if you're quiet.**
. . .
Almost /
inaudible.

CHRISTMAS:
Great.
Very good.
"Wicked, wicked eyes!"
NATHANIEL:
Yeah . . .

CHRISTMAS:
"You'll never see,
**You'll never know my shame,**
Go dark for all time,
**Blind to what you should never
have seen!"**
Nate? One of the books—I
just—says that Laius cursed
his whole family by stealing
somebody's son and raping him—
**Do you think Oedipus is cursed
because of that?**

PAOLA:
**Nate was very successful
when we met. He'd just
made *Cold Kisses*.**

FANNY:
**He directed that? Nate?**

PAOLA:
**He had a big development contract
at FOX, and convinced the studio to
use me in this big period piece
instead of I-won't-say-who but—**

FANNY:
Who who who who who
who who who who?
PAOLA:
Here's a picture of
what I looked like
before the Crixivan
started working its
wonders.

NATHANIEL:
**Sure, life ain't fair, what the hell.**
CHRISTMAS:
Cool.

"Blind to what you should
never have known.
This chant goes up:

'**Loved** her, **loved** her,'
Each time striking
again deep into
his eyes, dripping,
oozing bloody
muck, it's caught in
his beard,

FANNY:
**You're still beautiful.**
PAOLA:
**Oh go on. Anyway, they make [you]—**

FANNY:
*You are.*

PAOLA:
**Thank you.**
**You have to get a physical**
**when you're going to be**
**in a big movie—**

'**Loved** her,
**loved** her.'
He falls upon her:
the couple—a coupled
punishment upon
a coupled sin,
such happiness.

Once.
Now:

**Catastrophe!**
Throw wide the doors,
let all Thebes
see the father-killer,
the mother—

FANNY:
**Sure.**

PAOLA:
**—so we got my blood results back,**
**blah, blah, the whole thing fell apart,**
**Nate's big chance, he blames me;**
**I got pneumonia, pretty much**
**you name it, I got it, we fled**
**Hollywood, thank god Nate**
**had a private income, my**
**mother came out to take**
**care of me, she blames**
**Nate**
**who conveniently started**
**spiraling downward, buying**

| CHRISTMAS *(cont.)*: | PAOLA *(cont.)*: |
|---|---|
| too rank to say. | **drinks, drugs, sampling** |
| 'I AM THE PLAGUE! | **everything; then the** |
| I AM THE PLAGUE | **antivirals came along,** |
| I AM THE PLAGUE' | **I came along, twelve steps,** |
| He is spent—Well—" | **you know, then we decided** |
| | **we'd rather drink, he got** |
| | **the job at Harvard, but—** |

NATHANIEL: Okay, let's go back.

CHRISTMAS: I know you're going to fire me at the last minute.

NATHANIEL: You can't get out of it that easily.

JEN: Has Paola helped you at all?

HAKIJA: With? . . .

JEN: I'm so happy right now.

*(Hakija kisses Jen's breast through her blouse. They slip out of sight during:)*

PAOLA: . . . his confidence was . . . Scarily so. I mean, like a little child. And, well, he was hearing voices, for a while. *(Pause)* No longer, but . . . this is his first venture back into the world; it's a much bigger deal than he lets on.

*(Short pause.)*

FANNY: Didn't you want to play Jocasta?

PAOLA: Oh, god no. I think I've had enough of acting. *(Pause)* That's all you have to say, after what I told you?

FANNY: I, I don't know what else to—

PAOLA: It's okay.

FANNY: Sorry.

PAOLA: No, I like that you never seem to have a hidden agenda.

FANNY: You mean I'm incapable of censoring myself.

PAOLA: Well, I like that, too.

*(Pause.)*

CHRISTMAS: You never ever *ever ONCE* slept with a guy?

NATHANIEL: Okay, once.

CHRISTMAS: Oh, tell me, please? *Please?*

*(Beat.)*

NATHANIEL: When Paola and I met, she was absolutely sure I was gay, she still is.

CHRISTMAS: Yeah?

NATHANIEL: Don't ask, anyway, she kept saying, You should try it, you should try it, I think she just didn't want to be with one more guy who turned out to be bi, is my theory, she was testing me, so to finally I just to shut her up said, Okay, I will prove to you I'm not gay, and there was this admittedly rather hunky guy in the cast, and I went right up to him on closing night and said, My wife thinks you're hot, do you want to sleep with us, and we both had seen him eyeing me, I wasn't taking any chances of being rejected—

CHRISTMAS: I would never reject you.

NATHANIEL: —and the guy says, Sure, and we take eight tabs of ecstasy or whatever and we all hop into . . . well, the floor, and sure enough I am completely incapable of getting hard, though this guy works so diligently on me I'm still replacing skin he took off . . .

CHRISTMAS: Is that who infected her?

NATHANIEL: *Where is everybody?* We're not on a break, guys. Jen, Hak?

PAOLA: They're . . . / I just—

*(Jen and Hakija appear.)*

NATHANIEL: Okay, let's look at that foretelling, what is it, prophecy . . .

PAOLA: Anybody want anything?

NATHANIEL: Don't go too far. *(To Jen)* Go. Anytime.

JEN: Uh ... "Hear me now!

Why should any man fear the gods if chance is all there is?

There is no foretelling, no prophesying anything.

Better to live one's life without fear.

All men—"

NATHANIEL: I'm Oedipus, make *me* believe—

JEN: Okay.

NATHANIEL:

—change my mind.

JEN:

Okay.

"Hear me now!

FANNY:

**Why do you think ... ?**

**Is it ... possible that Paola and**

**I were the only two complete dunder-**

**heads left in all of Boston and**

**Cambridge who were actually willing**

**to play Elders in this turkey?**

Why should

any man fear the

gods if chance is all

there is? Chance!

There is no foretelling,

no prophesying

anything ... All

HAKIJA:

**Probably / not.**

men lie with

their mothers

in their dreams ...

Those who

FANNY:

**No. So ... Why do you think I ...**

**mean, Nate's a smart guy, don't**

**you ... ?**

give it no

more thought

are the happiest!"

HAKIJA:

**Nate?**

NATHANIEL:

I'm unconvinced.

FANNY:

**Right?**

JEN:

Oh.

HAKIJA:

**Sure.**

Okay.

FANNY:
**Why would he do such a thing?**

HAKIJA:
**You tell me.**


FANNY:
**Because...**
...
**It's almost impossible.**

HAKIJA:
**Right.**

FANNY:
**And...**
...
**Ohhhh.**

HAKIJA:
**What?**

FANNY:
**Thank you.**


HAKIJA:
**I didn't do / anything...**

FANNY:
**Oh yes you did.**
**You're the only other person**
**around here who's devious enough**
**to have figured it out.**

NATHANIEL:
Me.
It's not about you.

JEN:
"Hear me now.
Why should any
man fear the
gods if
chance
is all there
is...?
...
There is no
foretelling,
no prophesying
anything.
Better to
live one's
life without
fear."


NATHANIEL:
Sorry.
...
Look, I'm not trying
to drive you crazy...


**You *love* him. You**

NATHANIEL *(cont.)*:
**want to save his
life!**

**. . .**

HAKIJA:
I don't know what you're—

**. . .**

**You *fuck* him.
Maybe I'd believe
it more if you'd
waited until opening
night.**

FANNY:
Shut up. I mean, thanks.

JEN:
**What?**

PAOLA:
/ Nate.

NATHANIEL *(To Jen)*:
Why do you say every line as if you
want me to feel sorry for you? Is
that what you learned at Yale? I
don't remember that. She is
determined to get what she wants,
which is not my pity.

We haven't—

PAOLA:
Nate.

No. Of course.

NATHANIEL:
Cry all you want, cry
cry—
Fine, good, but sooner or later
you are going to have to make these
scenes about the person you are
playing to and not yourself
and your exquisite and
sensitive feelings . . .
Good. Because nobody cares how
deep we are, any of us. The only

. . . I—know—

**. . .**

I'm not crying.

I know. I agree.

NATHANIEL *(cont.)*:
thing anyone cares about is what people
do and how they do it, not what they feel.
You feel too much.

PAOLA: That's e / nough—

JEN: / It's okay.

NATHANIEL: I care— *(To Paola)* Do you want to direct the play?
*(To Jen)* I care what Jocasta *wants* or how she goes about
trying to get it.

JEN: Me, too. *(Pause)* Me, too. I'll get it.

NATHANIEL: Well, day before opening is getting a little late for
promises. [Wouldn't you say?]

### SCENE 5

*Opening night. A communal dressing room. All six.*

FANNY: You want to know what my tragedy was?, I know we
weren't supposed to tell: Instead of being born who I am in
1972, I'm born in ancient Greece and my name is Medea.

STAGE MANAGER'S VOICE *(Over a loudspeaker)*: Five minutes,
ladies and gentlemen, this is five minutes to places.

FANNY: Oh god, baby Jesus.

CHRISTMAS: This is a pagan play. No Jesus.

JEN: You want to hear something beautiful? "We learn to give
way. For winter storms step aside for summer, terrible
storms tame the sea to calm, and the prison of sleep—"

| FANNY *(Sings)*: | JEN: |
|---|---|
| "To everything, turn turn turn." | "—eventually frees all those jailed within." |
| *(Fanny starts to whistle;* | NATHANIEL: |
| *several actors shush her.)* | Do I look as much like Elmer Fudd in this as I think? |

PAOLA:
No! Whistling!
Spit and turn around three times.      JEN:
Do it! / Spit and turn around—          "Should we never learn our
turn around—                            place or come to wisdom?
                                        I for one shall learn . . ."
FANNY: No. I won't. / No. No. Too bad. Bad luck. Tra la. Macbeth,
    Macbeth, Macbeth, Macbeth!
NATHANIEL: Listen, I want you to concentrate on what is at stake.
    Always, every moment, how high are the stakes for your
    character at each / and [every]—
STAGE MANAGER'S VOICE: Five minutes, ladies and gentlemen.
FANNY: We did that.
STAGE MANAGER'S VOICE: I'm sorry, make that places!

*(Paola exits.)*

My last call was late. / Sorry.
FANNY: Now s/he tells us that?
JEN: Break a leg.

*(She leaves.)*

NATHANIEL: Stakes!

*(Nathaniel exits, chanting "stakes, stakes, stakes!")*

CHRISTMAS: I want everyone to promise to be my friend no mat-
    ter how many dead whale dicks I suck tonight.
FANNY: I promise. And I hope you do, I hope everyone sucks, so
    I can stand out in bright relief.

*(Fanny and Christmas exit. Hakija closes his eyes. Fanny
returns and sees Hakija cross himself.)*

Blind Tereisias forgot his staff.

*(She exits. Pause. Music can be heard through the speakers; the audience grows quiet. Hakija exits. We watch the empty dressing room as, over the loudspeaker, we hear the curtain rise, then:)*

HAKIJA'S VOICE: "My children, why are you here, pleading, bent down?
The city is burdened with moans and incense, intertwined,
I would not trust a messenger, so I've come to hear with my own ears.
Priest, you speak for them?"

CHRISTMAS' VOICE: "Our ship, the city of Thebes,
Our city, the *ship* of Thebes,
Can barely lift her prow from these bloody waves:
Plague dragging our people, drowning them in death.
You saved our city once.
You rid *us of* the cursed Sphinx
Some say with the help of the gods,
We beseech you, help us once more.
If you don't, you will rule over an empty city."

*(Lights go to black, then bump right up again, mercilessly bright, and we are now onstage.)*

HAKIJA: "They said I should kill my father!
But he's dead, deep in the soil,
And here I stand, never laying a hand on him!
Unless he died longing for me.
I am not his killer!"

JEN: "I told you this."

HAKIJA: "I was too filled with fear to hear you.
But wait—mustn't I now fear my mother's bed?"

JEN: "Hear me now!
Why should any man fear the gods if chance is all there is?
Chance!

There is no foretelling, no prophesying anything.
Better to live one's life without fear.
All men lie with their mothers—in their dreams!
Those who give it no more thought than that are the
happiest."

*(Jump to:)*

PAOLA AND FANNY: "Add all the lives of all the generations who
have lived and died,
Add to these our own, and still you will come up with nothing.
Has there ever been a mortal whose joy was more than fantasy,
A vision born then snatched into oblivion before you blink?
You, Oedipus, are the shining example!
You stood above all men: your happiness all-encompassing.
And now is there a man in greater agony?
More joined forever to suffering, frenzy, panic?
Your life's triumphs ground to nothing—chaos."

*(Jump to:)*

CHRISTMAS: "'I AM THE PLAGUE!
I AM THE PLAGUE!
I AM THE PLAGUE!'
He is spent. Well . . . you may see for yourselves.
Look: the gates are opening."

*(Doors open center where we see the body of Jocasta. From the
shadows steps the blinded Oedipus.)*

HAKIJA: "Oh . . . Oh . . . Where am I going? Which way does my
voice go on that wind—[and] how far have these spirits
sprung? Dark—a nightmare dark, some fierce wind sting-

ing me with nothing but evil of my own deeds. The gods brought this bitterness to its conclusion, but the hand that struck me was my own. And why not? What was there left to see? With what eyes should I look upon my father's face in Hades, my mother? Would the sight of my own children bred as brothers, sisters bring light— These eyes were worthless before I rendered them so. Drive out the criminal, drive out the plague! I cursed myself with the curse of the gods. Time's tragic lesson: no mortal creatures *ever* win . . . all borne out before these eyes unseeing . . . Where are they? Look on me, bear witness, I cannot, I see too much to ever see again. If there were means to cut off my hearing I would, give me a knife, I'll cut into those membranes as well. Give it to me! . . . Apollo! Look now! I did what I came to do! Release me! I gave you your bidding so you might see how shameful, small, and soiled is man. I served my purpose, and am of no use to anyone . . . Like these putrid jellied eyes, smashed eggs . . . Did they fall? Sweep them away: crushed vermin, stabbed, bloody, blinded in God's name. *Hide me!* I beg you! Look to it! Let no one see. Kill me, smash me on rocks in some festering brine, wash me away! Don't touch me. No one but I can bear this. No one . . . Not even I . . . But I . . . No one . . . This doom . . . this shame. It is my own."

*(End of* Oedipus Tyrannus.*)*

### SCENE 6

*Opening night party.*

| FANNY: | CHRISTMAS: |
| --- | --- |
| YES!!! | Who was that fucking weirdo in the front row with the sparkly glasses? |

CRAIG LUCAS

NATHANIEL:
That's why I didn't want to limit it!
Yes, all of those interpretations are
valid and they're all there, you don't
have to pick one over the other—In fact,
if you do that, you don't allow the
audience to have their own, I mean,
you have to trust them, audiences are
smarter than we give them credit for.

JEN:
Oh oh oh!
*(To Hakija)*
**Tell them!**
Tell the—! Oh—

FANNY:
Glasses?

FANNY:
The kelp,
you mean?

CHRISTMAS:
He was fast
asleep.

PAOLA:
I saw him.

CHRISTMAS:
You did?

PAOLA:
That was
my agent.

CHRISTMAS:
No! Really? Oh.

HAKIJA:
**/ What?**

JEN:
**Your theory! About Oedipus and
the U.S.!**

HAKIJA:
**Oedipus and . . . Oh! No.**

JEN:
**Yes. Hak was saying, this was like
weeks ago, that he saw— You say it.**

FANNY:
Christmas gave me an
ecstasy, do you want one?

PAOLA:
No. *Oh, don't give
Nate one, please.*

FANNY:
You sure?

HAKIJA: I said that the U.S. reminds me of Oedipus—you made
your place in the world by native wit alone, and proved you
deserve to be number one.

NATHANIEL: That's very interesting.

FANNY: You hate that sort of interpretation.

JEN: No, but. I don't remember that good stuff about America,
though, I thought—

CHRISTMAS:
That's because he knows he's
talking to a Republican.
JEN:
Who's a *Republican*?

PAOLA:
St. Paul de Vence,

*(Christmas points to Nathaniel.)*

You are not.
CHRISTMAS: Smile!

*(Christmas takes a photograph of Jen in shock; he continues taking photos throughout.)*

FANNY: Thank you, now I'm blind.

JEN: Well then I'll tell you what he really said. He said we make ourselves willfully blind to our power, we can't afford to see that we're the ones making the world unlivable, we blame everyone and anyone but ourselves, "Oh, they hate us because we're free, we have a Democracy."

NATHANIEL: And it's true.

JEN:
**The rest of the world knows very well what we've done—**

CHRISTMAS:
You were both
really good, I
watched during
all my times

NATHANIEL:
**Help them time and time and time again, you mean?** / At our own expense?

offstage which
as you know
are frequent.

JEN:
**By being the world's foremost exporter of weapons?**
Can I have another? Thank you.

. . .
That horrible man
who fell asleep
through my speeches

97

JEN *(cont.)*:
...
*Republican?*

NATHANIEL:
Why is it that
some Americans
can only see evil—why
is it always the U.S.,
somehow the rest of the
the world, it's like they're
all these sweet little
baby deer and we're
the wolves—/Always.

JEN:
I'm not saying that.

NATHANIEL:
Hear me out. If we didn't
produce weapons and have
such strong defense, I can
promise, you would
be captive in some
Arabian cave, if they hadn't
already raped you and fed
you to their camels.

JEN:
Are you a racist too, Nate?

PAOLA:
Whoa whoa whoa, party,
everyone!

JEN:
Do you come from a lot of
money / or something?

CHRISTMAS *(cont.)*:
woke up for you!

FANNY *(To Hakija)*:
**You listen to me, all right? ... Don't
fuck with her. Jen. I'm totally—**

HAKIJA:
**/ Don't ... ?**

FANNY *(Over him, not stopping)*:
**Hey. I'm not that drunk, or even drunk.
Yet. So, just because everybody
loves you and I love you, too, I do, I
think you're great, and but I want you
to know that that doesn't mean you
can use her and walk away or some—**

HAKIJA:
**I / think—**

FANNY:
**No, no, I have more, and you listen.
She's been exploited before. If you
are just hoping to become a citizen
or something,
you have to prove yourself
worthy of her, she is better
than the rest of us—**

HAKIJA:
**I couldn't agree more.**

FANNY:
**As long as we're clear.
Because, if she weren't so great,**

PAOLA:
Scads. *Piles.* / *Oodles.*
Mountains.
NATHANIEL:
We were comfortable.
JEN:
Only rich people say that:
*comfortable.*
FANNY:
I think I have.
Is that—?
CHRISTMAS: Oh, this is so fun!
FANNY: Is that / the one—?

FANNY *(cont.)*:
**I would have fucked you in a**
**heartbeat, so there.**

CHRISTMAS:
*(Shouting)* Hey!
**Hey everybody!**
**...**
**Has anybody ever**
**played Yes or No?**
PAOLA:
Yes or No?

CHRISTMAS: Listen up, everybody, we're going to play this game!
FANNY: Listen!
PAOLA: / I hate games.

*(Ad lib responses during:)*

CHRISTMAS: Okay, all you can do is answer Yes or No. There's no Maybes, no, welllll, no explaining. Somebody starts, asks somebody a question, they say Yes or No, and then that person gets to ask anyone else a question. But—
NATHANIEL: Are we trying to—?
CHRISTMAS: To?
NATHANIEL: Guess something?
CHRISTMAS: No no no!
NATHANIEL: / What's—?
CHRISTMAS: Oh, listen, the most important thing, and we have to swear: nothing that's said ever leaves this room. You can't play if you don't promise.

99

NATHANIEL:
No surer way to guarantee the
dissemination of a rumor than
to ask for secrecy.
...
I swear!

FANNY:
We promise!

CHRISTMAS:
Does everybody swear to
keep whatever is said in this
/ room in this room?

PAOLA:
He's got his fingers crossed!

*(Ad lib responses: "Yes, I promise,"
"We swear!," etc.)*

NATHANIEL: All right, all right, I swear.

CHRISTMAS: Okay, who wants to go first?, me! This is just to skip to the chase, because usually everybody starts with these nice, bland questions and it takes a while till everybody gets bored enough to start / asking really interesting questions so I thought I'd start.

FANNY: Just ask the question!

CHRISTMAS: Nate: When you called, said Merry Christmas, that time, to me, were you saying that I was a big girl and too slight onstage like Mary, M-A-R-Y?

NATHANIEL: What?

CHRISTMAS: Were you saying M-A-R-Y Christmas?

NATHANIEL: No. Jesus. All this time / you've been ... ?

CHRISTMAS: Okay. Thank you. It's all right. Just a question.

NATHANIEL: Awwww. Dooo—oh ... ??? *(To Jen)* Did you vote in the last election?

JEN:
Ummm—

FANNY:
Tell the / truth.

PAOLA:
Like a dog
with a bone.
You!

JEN: I'm thinking, I'm thinking. When was the last election? No.

NATHANIEL: Ah-ha! / Armchair radical.

JEN: I confess, yes. You're right. Are ... *(To Hakija)* You really in love with me?

HAKIJA: Yes.

CHRISTMAS:
Awwwwww, how
sweet is that?

PAOLA:
No hesitation, how about that?

NATHANIEL: Well, what is he gonna say in front of all of us?

CHRISTMAS: Well, does that mean you *were* saying I'm a big girl?

HAKIJA:
*(To Jen)* Did you know—
. . .
Did you know your friend Fanny
was going to come to me tonight
and warn me not to hurt you—?

FANNY:
Nobody's asked me a single
question!

JEN: She did?

HAKIJA: Did you put her up to it?

JEN: She did?

CHRISTMAS: Yes or No.

JEN: Really?

CHRISTMAS: Guess that's a No.

JEN: Seriously?

FANNY:
Yes. So, Nate,
diiid you really—
Too bad, you asked a question,
did you cast only two Elders so Paola
would be so busy figuring out a way to
solve the problem she wouldn't be able
to become a backseat director?

JEN:
That wasn't my question.

NATHANIEL:
Did she tell you that?

PAOLA:
*What?!*

FANNY: Yes or No.

NATHANIEL: Yes. Did you . . . come up with that?

FANNY: No. / Just a guess—

PAOLA: Wait wait wait—

NATHANIEL: It's not your turn.

FANNY: Uhhh, Hak— Do atheist Muslims usually cross themselves like Christians?

HAKIJA: Sometimes—I—

FANNY:

Yes or No.  HAKIJA:  NATHANIEL:  PAOLA:
I said usually.  Yes,  I'm kidding!  Backseat
  I suppose.    director . . .

CHRISTMAS: They do?

HAKIJA: No. Not / usually.

FANNY: Before the show, he did. "Father, Son, and Holy Ghost." To the correct side even. / I caught you!

PAOLA:  FANNY:
Any superstition will do,  Closet Christian.
at that point.

HAKIJA: Paola, do you think that Nate knows [you]— No, no, I can't.

FANNY: Too late, / you have to say it.

HAKIJA: No.

PAOLA: Go ahead, I what?

CHRISTMAS: Ask something else.

NATHANIEL: / No, go ahead.

CHRISTMAS: It's just a game, guys, this isn't approved by the American Psychiatric Association, okay?

NATHANIEL: Ask your question.

HAKIJA: Does Nate know you were working with many of the actors in secret?

PAOLA:

Oh, come on—No.  NATHANIEL:
That's like, "Why do you beat  Yes or No?
your wife?" I did a little coaching.
I did some coaching.

NATHANIEL: Yes. Is the answer.

PAOLA: Yes. *(Pause)* You're making it sound like / a big deal.

NATHANIEL:
I'll take one of those ecstasies.
Thank you.

CHRISTMAS:
Really?
Well, I don't...

NATHANIEL:
It's not addictive.
And I don't need a coach.
Yes. Thanks for the
offer. It'll be fine.

PAOLA:
No.
...
Honey, please—
...
That's ridiculous—
Punish me—
not yourself.

CHRISTMAS: Let's all take off our clothes or play another game at least.

PAOLA: You don't really care that I helped people, do you? / It wasn't—directing, I wasn't—

NATHANIEL: No. Would you be even capable of seeing my casting two people as the Chorus as a compliment, the idea that you could actually solve that, and brilliantly, *if* it were true I done that?

CHRISTMAS:
If? You keep doing that!

PAOLA:
Yyyyyyes...
and
No.

FANNY:
Shhh.

FANNY:
Yes or No.

CHRISTMAS:
Seriously.

PAOLA: What are you, the game police? No. Did you?

NATHANIEL: No. Jen: Would, let's see, being a huge, highly paid, much admired, award-winning, healthy, slim, ever-young, world-traveling movie star make you happier than having a loving home with a husband who genuinely adored you and a beautiful, healthy child to call your own?

JEN: No.

FANNY:
Ooooo.

CHRISTMAS:
I believe her.
... I want a child ...

HAKIJA:
Jen's turn ...

God.

JEN: Um ...
PAOLA: I'm sorry, honey.
NATHANIEL: I'm fine.
PAOLA: All right. *(Pause)* Ask if—
FANNY: Let her do it.
PAOLA: All right.

*(Pause.)*

JEN:
I'm thinking ...

CHRISTMAS:
Anything. Off the top of your head.

HAKIJA:
*(Mouthed to Jen, who looks at him)* What?

*(Pause.)*

NATHANIEL: Don't even think about it, just ...

*(Pause.)*

FANNY: Anything.
PAOLA: Let her do it!

*(Fanny sticks out her tongue; Paola sticks out her tongue; the two kiss.)*

## SCENE 7

JEN *(To us)*: Nate was good for his word; in no time at all Hak found an agent, changed his name and abandoned economics for New York. Fanny and Paola . . . fall in love. They're both sober and live in Northampton where they run a ski shop in winter and a landscape business in the summer; they're adopting a Chinese baby. Christmas works for them and rents an apartment in their house. Nate and Paola are no longer friends. He has returned to New York and found work directing . . . a soap opera. He lives down the hall and is our closest friend.

*(The sound of a baby crying.)*

That's Naomi. She's seven months and three days old. Hak and I are discussing maybe having one more.

*(Pause; the baby continues crying.)*

Oh, I let her cry; I know when she's hungry or needs to be changed, and she usually stops in a minute or two. I know some people disagree with that, but A) I'm not some people, B) She's one of the happiest and easiest babies I've ever known, and C) Fuck them with their unsolicited opinions.

*(The baby has stopped crying.)*

See? *(Beat)* Hak has a scene today and tomorrow with Robert De Niro in an independent film about—*guess what!*—the Mafia! Life is nothing if not predictable. If you know how to read all the clues and take the time to put them together. I was never one to do my homework . . .

*(Intercom buzzes. She moves to it. Into the intercom:)*

Yes?

CHRISTMAS: Hey, Jen, it's Chris ... Christmas? And—/ Fanny and Paola?

JEN: Oh, hiiiiii! Come on in. My god.

*(She buzzes them in. She opens the door.)*

Oh my god.

FANNY: Surprise.

JEN: I can't believe it. The Messenger, the Prophet, the Elders!

*(Christmas, Paola, and Fanny enter the apartment; they are in winter garb.)*

JEN: How are you? What a treat, wow.

CHRISTMAS: Is Hak here?

JEN: No, he's working. Take off your coats.

PAOLA: Hey, baby.

JEN: He'll be sorry to miss you, what's going on?

FANNY: We're Christmas shopping.

CHRISTMAS: I said you'd be home, we took a chance.

JEN: I'm glad.

CHRISTMAS: You look great.

JEN:
So do you, all of you, my god. Your hair!

PAOLA:
I know.

CHRISTMAS:
Where's all that fat you're supposed to have after having a baby?

JEN:
You look fantastic.
You do. Oh.
All of you.
You can look. Go on in.

PAOLA:
Is she, is she asleep?

*(Paola and Christmas exit.)*

FANNY: How are you?
JEN: I'm good. Do you want to see?
FANNY: I don't want to wake her.
JEN: You won't.

*(Fanny exits as Christmas reappears.)*

JEN: Are you well?
CHRISTMAS: It's good to see you.
JEN: Oh, you, too. Is everything . . . ? I mean.
CHRISTMAS: We're fine, we're good.
JEN: I'm sorry Hak isn't here.

*(Pause.)*

CHRISTMAS: Great place.
JEN: Oh, I forgot you hadn't seen it.
CHRISTMAS: Fabulous. Really. I, hey, is that your voice on the mayonnaise commercial?
JEN: It is.
CHRISTMAS: I knew it! I hear you a lot, I think.
JEN: Yeah, that's been good. And I can take Naomi with me, usually, sometimes I get a sitter. Nate, actually.
CHRISTMAS: Townsende?
JEN: He lives down the hall.

CHRISTMAS: Oh my god, don't tell . . .

JEN: I won't. I can make a pot of coffee.

CHRISTMAS: I'm good. Thanks.

JEN: So . . . god . . . Well, do you miss it? Acting?

CHRISTMAS: Oh, no, I, you know?, always felt like I was standing up there in a sundress with a big wet lollipop. I wanted to . . . *act*, really act, be active the world in ways that would make it better or at least try / to.

| JEN: | |
|------|------|
| Great. That's | CHRISTMAS: |
| wonderful. | Yeah. |

*(Paola and Fanny reenter.)*

PAOLA: Oh my god what?

CHRISTMAS: What?

PAOLA: Oh, please. Oh my god what? [I heard someone say . . . ]

JEN: Nate lives right down the hall. Two apartments over.

PAOLA: I'm gonna be sick.

JEN: I'm sorry. I would have told you if you'd called.

PAOLA: I don't want to know how he is unless he's really awful.

JEN: Okay. Fair enough.

PAOLA: He's not?

FANNY: . . . She looks so much like you.

CHRISTMAS *(To Paola)*: Breathe.

JEN: You think? I can only see Hak. Around the mouth? *(Pause.)* Can I get you anything? Tea? Coffee? No? Are you drinking?

CHRISTMAS: Not officially.

JEN: Ah-ha. Oh, he's going to be heartbroken he missed you, you're welcome to hang around. *(Pause)* Did you see him on *Law and Order*? His accent's almost gone, he's been working with a dialect coach. *(Pause)* Okay, what's going on?

FANNY: We missed you.

CHRISTMAS: Nothing.

*(Short pause.)*

JEN: Okay.

PAOLA: Okay, you can tell me, what's he doing?

JEN: Nate? He's subbing on a soap.

PAOLA: Which?

JEN: *Betrayals.*

PAOLA: Oh good.

JEN: Why?

PAOLA: It stinks. Serves him right.

JEN: Oh. You're right it does. But . . . well.

PAOLA: Is he seeing anyone?

JEN: We see him most nights.

PAOLA: Oh, so he's seeing you. Are you all having sex?

JEN: He's straight.

PAOLA: I'll be the judge of that, thank you. I know he thinks I left him because of Fanny, but that isn't why. I left him because I had to take care of him and I was the one who was sick.

JEN: . . . Uh-huh.

PAOLA: And at some point during our play, I started to feel . . .

JEN: You don't have to justify yourself.

PAOLA: Maybe I do. Rehearsing is about cooperation, collaboration—

JEN: Uh-huh.

PAOLA: —not dictatorship. And all that process bullshit.

JEN: / I—

PAOLA: He scapegoated you!

JEN: / Well—

PAOLA: Terribly. And look how many of us quit acting after that production, half!

JEN: I don't—He helped me in the part, I felt; he brought Hak and me together, so . . . I have, obviously, very different feelings. *(Silence)* I'm sorry it was so hard.

PAOLA: I lucked out. I'm not complaining.

*(Pause.)*

JEN: Why don't you stay for dinner? I'll send out—
CHRISTMAS: Well, no, we wanted to . . .
JEN: Are you sure? Oh. What?
CHRISTMAS: See you, you know, just you.
JEN: Oh. Why?
CHRISTMAS: Well . . .
JEN: Something's wrong. Isn't it?

*(Paola, Fanny and Christmas look at one another.)*

*What?*
PAOLA: We weren't sure you'd be alone.
CHRISTMAS: We didn't want to just call you up or send a letter.
JEN: All right.
FANNY: We thought you should have friends with you when . . .
JEN: When what?

*(Short pause.)*

CHRISTMAS: I . . .
JEN: What?
FANNY: We have been seriously debating whether or not we should even do this.
JEN: Do what?
CHRISTMAS: I went to Hak's hometown.
JEN: In Bosnia?
CHRISTMAS: Yes. Through my church, I'm Unitarian now, I got involved in food distribution and . . . I went over twice, actually.
JEN: Wow.
CHRISTMAS: The second time I . . .
JEN: That's . . . [wonderful?]

CHRISTMAS: ... because we all loved him, we were all so close, and he was such an inspiration to all of us— I don't know, I wanted to see his home. Or ...

JEN: Uh-huh.

CHRISTMAS: Everything's been partitioned ...

JEN: Yes.

CHRISTMAS: And but many people are returning. A surprising [number]. The trials, I think, at the Hague—

JEN: Uh-huh.

CHRISTMAS: —are encouraging people, or are going to, anyway ...

JEN: What's it ...? Tell me.

CHRISTMAS: I asked around about Hak, and told everyone I knew him and ... I got a ... strange ... Everyone said he was dead.

*(Short pause.)*

JEN: Why?

CHRISTMAS: Well, I said, No, I know him, he's told me all about the town, and I described him, I—and everyone said, No, Hakija Osmonovic looked nothing like that, he was not tall, he and his family were killed on the same day ... *(Pause)* And I left.

FANNY: We weren't going to do anything.

CHRISTMAS: And ... I took a few names, said I would write. I ... copied a few photos of Hak and sent them over ... I was ... concerned, I don't know.

JEN: Uh-huh.

CHRISTMAS: And everyone I sent them to wrote back, individually, maybe they ... They said the man in the photograph was a Bosnian Serb, from that town, who had participated in the ...

*(Pause.)*

JEN: / I don't—

PAOLA: He'd been part of the massacres. He was particularly—
JEN: Thank you. *(Short pause)* Yes.

*(Pause.)*

CHRISTMAS: You don't want to know?
FANNY: Everyone said—
JEN: Thank you. / That's . . .
FANNY: —he was one of the ringleaders, one of the most brutal,
a / rapist.
JEN: That's enough. *(Pause)* I wonder if I can get my money back.
Do they do that with babies?

*(Short pause.)*

CHRISTMAS: I wrote back again and said it couldn't be him. Not
possible.

*(Silence.)*

FANNY: We were sent . . .

*(She produces a videotape.)*

CHRISTMAS: I said we shouldn't come.
FANNY: I'm sorry.
JEN: Keep it. Take it.

*(Pause.)*

FANNY: You can throw it away if you / don't— You don't have to
look at it.
JEN: True. Okay. Well. Merry Christmas.
CHRISTMAS: Should we not have told you—. . . ?

JEN: Don't give it another thought, flee.

PAOLA: Watch the tape.

JEN: How could I dare to be happy? / Is that ...?

FANNY: You know this has nothing to do with that.

JEN: Would you have told him? To his face? If he'd been here. Would you?... *Would you?!*

PAOLA: I would.

FANNY: We just didn't want you living with someone who might...

JEN: Well, I'm sure you're right. Good luck with your new child, I hope she works out—her father doesn't turn out to be some kind of war criminal, / you'll have to—

FANNY: Stop.

*(Silence.)*

CHRISTMAS: Did you know already?

JEN: ... Good-bye.

CHRISTMAS: Did you?

FANNY: You know that we all love you very much. / And I'm—

| CHRISTMAS: | JEN: |
|---|---|
| We do, / baby. | Yes. |

FANNY: —concerned about you. That's all.

JEN: Are you going to, what, now, go to the relief agencies, denounce him?

CHRISTMAS: We would never—

JEN: You would never—What are the things you would never?

PAOLA: Watch that fucking tape, do you understand? We're not talking about plays and commercials and Robert De / fucking Niro—

FANNY: / Honey—Babe—

PAOLA: —we're talking about human beings, we're talking about savagery, you fucking little cow, how dare you act all huffy, he should be on trial!

CHRISTMAS: / Come on now.

PAOLA: You think all this is going under the rug, you fucking little—

*(Christmas tries to direct Paola toward the door.)*

Get your hands off, don't be such a *fairy*, both of you, I'm sick of all the nice nice, these are indecencies, / crimes against—!

FANNY'S VOICE: All right, baby.

PAOLA'S VOICE: Not all right, NOT.

FANNY'S VOICE: / Okay.

PAOLA'S VOICE: She should be begging, they both should— *God sees! For mercy!*

*(Time passes. The baby begins to cry; Jen disappears into the nursery. The crying stops. Pause. Hakija enters, and Jen emerges from the bedroom, freshly showered, her hair wet. She takes particular care to close the door all the way behind her; we hear it click under:)*

HAKIJA: Hey.

JEN: Welcome home.

*(They kiss. During the following, he is oblivious to Jen's manner.)*

HAKIJA: How was your day?

JEN: How was yours is the question?

HAKIJA: Oh, he's incredibly nice.

JEN: Bob?

HAKIJA: He really is. Very shy, sort of, sly—he has this smile that creeps up, I think to let you know that he's not an asshole or going to demand center stage—

You want a glass?

JEN: Sure.

HAKIJA: I really liked him, and the scene, I don't know, we'll see.

JEN: Thank you. Tchin-tchin.

HAKIJA: Tchin-tchin. Oh god, it was just . . . well, I mean, at the same time that I was thinking, you know, I can handle this, I've earned this, I've gotten myself here, nobody else has, I mean, we have, gotten ourselves here, but . . . it's not like, I don't know, I had to keep going, don't, you know, just play the scene, and then at the same time I couldn't, oh . . . It was crazy. You okay?

JEN: What else?

HAKIJA: He played off everything I gave him, he was very open, not bossy. At all. Almost, I don't know, it was fun. So. *(Notices the videotape)* What's this?

JEN: Came for you.

HAKIJA: What is it?

JEN: I haven't looked.

HAKIJA: Who sent it?

JEN: Put it in the machine.

HAKIJA: All right. You seem . . .

*(Hakija looks at the tape, inserts the tape into the VCR, turns on the TV. Hold, static, then the tape comes on—we do not see the screen. There is the laughter of men, then the sound of a woman begging in Serbo-Croatian, and the laughter grows more raucous. The woman screams, petrified. Hakija turns off the tape.)*

Where did you get that?

JEN: It was a gift.

HAKIJA: I see.

*(Silence.)*

There was no choice for us. When the Serbs came through, it was clear that we either participated or we were killed. I know this is very difficult for you to believe or to understand. Milosevic opened the prisons and made an army out of criminals, the most deranged and violent criminals he could find.

They drove all the efforts. One was either one of them or one was dead, those were the two choices. *(Silence)* There isn't anything . . . *(Silence)* You have no way of imagining. It was worse than a nightmare. I know you see me on the tape, but that's, if I didn't . . . if we didn't all play along . . .

There were only two choices. You think I'm proud of . . . Christ oh Christ. *(Pause)* Is Naomi sleeping? *(Silence)* Please, Jen. What do you want me . . . ? The war was ending . . . I took his passport, I hadn't killed him, but . . . I could have; it could have been anyone. We were, yes, I'd grown up with him; I had my picture attached to it; it wasn't difficult. I didn't want to be that man anymore. I promise you that I did not . . . *choose* . . .

*(Hakija rises moves to the bedroom door, tries it; it is locked.)*

. . . What did you do? *(Jiggles the lock harder)* Where's the key? Do you have it?

*(He throws his weight against the door; it does not budge; he hurls himself against it several times:)*

Naomi. Come on! Naomi!

*(He continues kicking it, slowly loosening the hinges, the lock, and with one final, violent kick, the door opens, and Hakija rushes in.)*

*(From off)* Where is she? *(Returns)* What have you done with her?

*(Jen picks up the phone and dials, waits a second.)*

What are you doing, where's Naomi? Please, Jen, please god—
JEN: Come on over.

*(She hangs up, opens the front door.)*

HAKIJA: Who is that? Don't torture me like this, I'll do whatever you want—

*(Nathaniel walks in with the baby in his arms.)*

NATHANIEL: Shh, I just got her to sleep, took forever. What's the matter? Should I . . . ?
JEN: Stay. Here.
NATHANIEL: What happened?
JEN: Ask him.
NATHANIEL: Did someone die?
JEN: Yes. Tell him. Tell him who died. I wanted you to know what it is like to lose a daughter. To not know where she was or what had happened to her, to fear the worst, if only for a few seconds.
HAKIJA: Thank you.
NATHANIEL: What happened?
JEN: We'll tell you. In time.
HAKIJA: Oh, thank you.
JEN: We'll tell you.
HAKIJA: Oh my god . . . I'm sorry, I'm sorry, thank you . . .
NATHANIEL: Jen?
JEN: "Time, the all-seeing, has found us out against our will."
HAKIJA: I'm so sorry . . . Thank you . . .
JEN *(To us)*: I knew what was on the tape without watching it. "Why should any man fear the gods if chance is all there is?

Better to live one's life without fear . . . Those who give it no more thought than that are the happiest." I remember that. I forget the rest. I don't believe in tragedy. Did you know that there is no other word for it in any other language, it is always a variant of the Greek word: tragedy. It belongs to them . . . I choose to be happy. To me Oedipus is a fool. I don't cry for him, I cringe. Jocasta, on the other hand, all she's trying to do is protect her marriage—her first by murdering the child who threatens it, and her second by hiding the truth from her husband, once she knows. I don't want to be Medea. I choose to be happy. You can do that. You really can. Hak still always says that Americans don't understand tragedy, and I hope that could always be true. Don't you? Well . . . God bless you. May He keep us all from harm. Goodnight.

END OF PLAY

*This is Christmas's audition scene, beginning on page 14. Christmas reads the Shepherd and Paola and Nathaniel read Oedipus and the Messenger.*

OEDIPUS: You! Ancient fellow, look me straight in the eye. Did you ever belong to King Laius?

SHEPHERD: I did—Born and raised in the palace, not purchased on the block.

OEDIPUS: What were your tasks?

SHEPHERD: Herding, / all my life.

OEDIPUS: Where? I didn't ask how long.

SHEPHERD: Cithaeron, the foothills.

OEDIPUS: Ever seen this man before?

SHEPHERD: No, I ... Wait ... my memory's going ...

MESSENGER: So many years we worked together, you don't remember me at all?

SHEPHERD: Maybe I do, don't rush me, everything was long ago.

MESSENGER: You don't remember giving me an infant to raise?

SHEPHERD: Shh, why dredge that up now?

MESSENGER: Here he is—look!

SHEPHERD: Shut your mouth, you need a thrashing!

OEDIPUS: You need the lash more than he, old fool.

SHEPHERD: Your majesty, what . . . ?

OEDIPUS: Answer his question!

SHEPHERD: Don't torment an old man, I'm begging you.

OEDIPUS: Twist his arm— / Hard!

SHEPHERD: No—God help me—

OEDIPUS: Did you give him a child?

SHEPHERD: I wish I'd died . . . instead . . .

OEDIPUS: You did?

SHEPHERD: The more I say, the more you'll torture me!

OEDIPUS *(To the Messenger)*: Harder! More!

SHEPHERD: Yes! YES! I did.

OEDIPUS: Where did you get this child?

SHEPHERD: No more—I can't remember—

OEDIPUS: Break his arm in two.

SHEPHERD: From the palace!

OEDIPUS: Slave or royalty?

SHEPHERD: I can't.

OEDIPUS: Cut him open!

SHEPHERD: It was his own son, Laius!

OEDIPUS: My wife? Gave you this wretched child?

SHEPHERD: Yes, my lord. To kill. I was to slay the babe.

OEDIPUS: Her own?

SHEPHERD: Yes! Yes. To foil the prophecy.

OEDIPUS: And you disobeyed? You dared to . . . ?

SHEPHERD: I am lost!

OEDIPUS: Lost! I'm lost—exposed. Cursed at birth, cursed in wedding, cursed a murder.

APPENDIX B

This insert begins on page 58 after Nathaniel's line: "I'm not being coy and ironic..."

NATHANIEL: If you were going, I were going to take a particular, you know, slant on the play—I mean, that would be the one I'd—and I'm *not* going to do that, I hate that in productions where you can see the goddamn point of view of the director like handprints from a blind person feeling their way around the set after they've fallen into paint: You see?, it's all about the "Riddle of Human Identity"—who are we? It's all about repression, *right????*, and the Freudians all leap up and cheer, or it's about rootlessness, the homeless! Oedipus, poor thing, is thrust out of his warm home as an infant no less and then he's thrust out again, for good, and blind no less, as an adult! Social workers, take note. And socialists. Or it's about the civilized versus the bestial, our cultural, learned behavior in opposition to the savage creature within who must then be cast out, the scapegoat, you see!

Tragedy itself, the word, is based on this: the goat! Goat festival, or some fucking thing, Paola can tell you. OR OR it's about pollution, inside and out, OR as some, one of us suggested Oedipus is Athens, read "America," get it?!?, or it's about the search for ultimate meaning, is suffering what gives us meaning or is it the search for meaning that causes us to suffer so much?!? OR, is it all some juridical debate as to which laws are still appropriate—all the ACLU-ers would line up around the block. That shit is easy! Oh, wow, he's saying is it a random universe or do the gods have a plan, no matter how inscrutable! You'd win an Obie for that. And and . . . I don't know . . . I'm . . .

*(At some point during this, Fanny responds to the conversation between Paola and Christmas about the women he's slept with. If it interrupts the above scene, then she returns to Nathaniel with a contrite expression, and he will have held, patiently, for her return.)*

CRAIG LUCAS

PLAYS: *Missing Persons, Reckless, Blue Window, Prelude to a Kiss, God's Heart, The Dying Gaul, Stranger, Prayer for My Enemy, The Singing Forest, The Lying Lesson, Ode to Joy, I Was Most Alive with You* and *Death of the Republic.*

SCREENPLAYS: *Longtime Companion, The Secret Lives of Dentists, Reckless, Blue Window, Prelude to a Kiss* and *The Dying Gaul.*

ENGLISH LANGUAGE ADAPTATIONS: *Miss Julie, Three Sisters, Uncle Vanya* and *Galileo.*

LIBRETTI: *The Light in the Piazza* (music and lyrics by Adam Guettel), *3 Postcards* (music and lyrics by Craig Carnelia), *Two Boys* (composer Nico Muhly, world premiere at the English National Opera; American premiere at the Metropolitan Opera), *Orpheus in Love* (composer Gerald Busby), *Amélie* (Dan Messe, composer and co-lyricist; Nathan Tysen, co-lyricist) and *Three Women* (based on Robert Altman's film; composer Gerald Busby).

DIRECTION: *The Light in the Piazza* (world premiere, Intiman Theater); *This Thing of Darkness* (co-authored with David Schulner, Atlantic Theater Company); *Saved Or Destroyed* (by Harry Kondoleon; Cherry Lane/Rattlestick) and *Play Yourself* (by Harry Kondoleon; NYTW); *Ode to Joy* (Rattlestick Theater); films *The Dying Gaul* and *Birds of America.*

AWARDS: Steinberg Best New Play Award (*The Singing Forest*), Laura Pels/PEN Mid-Career Award, NY Film Critics Best Screenplay (*The Secret Lives of Dentists*), Sundance Audience Award (*Longtime Companion*), Excellence in Literature Award from the American Academy of Arts and Letters, Greenfield Prize, three Obies (including one for his direction of *Saved or Destoyed* and two for Best Play for *Prelude to a Kiss* and *Small Tragedy*), LAMBDA Literary Award; Rockefeller, Guggenheim and NEA Fellowships; three Tony nominations; Pulitzer finalist.

CRAIG LUCAS's essays have appeared in numerous publications including the *New York Times*. He is currently writing a play about the 1960s for Arena Stage's Power Play Cycle. He lives in upstate New York with writer and visual artist Frankie KL.